NEVER GOOD WITH HORSES

SIMON ARMITAGE

# Never Good with Horses
*Assembled Lyrics*

faber

First published in 2023
by Faber & Faber Ltd
Bloomsbury House
74–77 Great Russell Street
London WC1B 3DA

Typeset by Faber & Faber Ltd
Printed in the UK by TJ Books Ltd, Padstow, Cornwall

A CIP record for this book
is available from the British Library

ISBN 978-0-571-37761-9

10 9 8 7 6 5 4 3 2 1

# CONTENTS

THE ULTRAVIOLET AGE

THREE WEATHER SONGS

LYR, PENDING

MISCELLANEOUS

# INTRO

Song lyrics are not poems and poems are not song lyrics.
Controversial? Song lyrics come packaged with an indefinable
and inexplicable element called music that can transform
the most mundane and seemingly innocuous phrase into
something memorable and ethereal. Throw in a vocal style
and a funky video, and the words of a song are reduced to a
small component part in a large and complex system. Poems,
at least those that earn their keep on the page, live and die
by the sequencing of (usually) black shapes on white paper,
and for the most part go about their business very quietly.
Any orchestration in a printed poem is entirely a matter of
letters and punctuation marks, with the visual component
restricted to aspects of typography, layout and paper quality
etc. However deeply song lyrics and poetry might share the
same origins back in the unknowable past, like pretty much
everything else in this world they have become specialisms
and disciplines in their own right. At the same time there is
a clear overlap, for example in the material used (language)
and the techniques at work (verse, rhyme, rhythm, repetition,
and so on). Performance poets and spoken word artists bridge
the gap between the two art forms, as do so-called page poets
when they take to the lectern or stage to give readings from
their books. As someone who usually writes poems for two-
dimensional surfaces but gives readings about once a week, and
as someone who writes lyrics for a band but only ever speaks
them, I've become very interested in that occluded territory
where songs and poems demonstrate their interconnectedness.
Poetry is the art form of absence: when I write a poem I'm
very conscious of deliberately leaving ideas out, ideas that will
be supplied by a reader. When I write a song lyric I'm also
leaving things out, but those omissions tend to be emotional

rather than intellectual, and will be filled by notes, chords, instruments. So issues of inclusion and exclusion also unite the two practises, even if the matter they create and the voids they open up appeal to different regions of the mind.

The pieces collected here cover many years and dozens of different projects. Right from the beginning of my 'career' as a poet I've been asked to write song lyrics now and again, and have always been willing to try my hand. In the early years I made occasional forays into the world of nineties pop-rock or whichever folk revival was taking place at the time, but always found myself down creative cul-de-sacs and artistic blind alleys. I've learned that in the music industry, the one thing that can't be relied on is the music industry. Time passed. The first song lyrics I penned that received any kind of public transmission or widespread dissemination were for television, in the unlikely category of documentary, with the films *Drinking for England, Feltham Sings* and *Songbirds*. Then in 2007 I co-founded the indie pop band the Scaremongers with singer-songwriter and occasional poet Craig Smith. In some ways it was the re-formation of a band we'd never got around to organising in the mid-eighties. Back then, after the weekly poetry workshop, we'd write songs together, trying to be Orange Juice or Felt or some other jangly floppy-fringed group of the era. Some of the lyrics in this volume go right back to those bedsit days in Huddersfield and Manchester (the gas-fire sessions!). Garage bands require garages, and neither his parents nor mine owned one. So we were a kitchen sink band, both by genre and by virtue of our songs being composed around the washing up bowl, and usually performed to an audience of dirty pots and pans. In our twenty-first century iteration we were still a DIY outfit, doing everything out of our own pocket and calling in as many favours as we could. We released one album, *Born in a Barn*, and several singles, on our own Corporation Pop 'label' (in Yorkshire the Local Authority was traditionally referred to as the Corporation, and Corporation Pop was a euphemism for water, especially for families not prepared to splash out on a bottle of Dandelion & Burdock or American Cream Soda). I don't look back on those experiences as a training session for what followed but I certainly learned lessons along the way. Lessons about not being too verbose or garrulous, for example. Readers can take their time over a poem, experience it at their own pace, but a song goes by at a fixed speed and listeners aren't given the opportunity to unpack dense metaphysical utterances or look up obscure references. Wordy songs can also become impossible tongue twisters, but the biggest issue with a long and linguistically extravagant song is that it's hard to remember. On several occasions when we played live I forgot the words – words I'd written! – and would either mumble complete gibberish in the hope of styling it out for a couple of bars, or turn away from the microphone as if overcome by transcendent guitar chords or rendered speechless by the trembling harmonics of the Hammond organ. I needn't have worried; language is somewhat sacrificial in the mouths of many singers, and even the most devoted music fans are perfectly happy not being able to decipher every word of their favourite songs. At the operatic end of the scale, the classically trained voice seems incapable of any lexical clarity whatsoever, contorting and deforming language to the point of incomprehensibility. It has been explained to me, several times and at great length, why such distortion is necessary if sopranos or tenors are to deliver perfect notes with feeling and volume. But I'm not buying it – it was never a problem for Sinatra. I could have published several libretti in this book and let my operatic characters and narrators be heard for the first time. But in the end I decided to stick with the shorter set-piece lyrics, the ones that look less like scripts, and more like, well, poems.

In 2010 the singer-songwriter Richard Walters got in touch to ask if I'd be interested in providing a lyric for him. He made a song version of my poem 'Redwoods', then sent me a hand-held recording device with the idea of generating new spoken-word pieces that might be developed into further material. The machine, with its furry grey microphone, sat on my desk for several months like a stuffed animal. Then one day I began looking through some of my old poems – odds and sods that had never really found a home in mainstream poetry collections, more extrovert and patterned than my usual work – and decided to reclassify them as lyrics. It was as much a psychological determination as a literary or musical one, but it proved something of a creative breakthrough, and eventually encouraged me to write new pieces that had the same kind of tone, or weight, or approach. A few months later we teamed up with producer and multi-instrumentalist (and mid-Devon cabin-dweller) Patrick James Pearson, and felt confident and enthusiastic enough about the enterprise to call ourselves a band, give ourselves the name Land Yacht Regatta, and sign a contract with a major label. We've jumped ship since then. If there's a second thing I've learned about the music industry, it's to still not rely on the music industry. But LYR are very much alive and kicking, and not just in terms of recording and releasing records, but through bespoke commissions and large-scale customised projects, two of which – in Durham and Barnsley – are represented in this book. When we began, LYR's ambition was to compose music in keeping with our 'ambient, post-rock' tag (whatever that means) and to perform in formal venues or at left-field festivals rather than in the upstairs of pubs. In the end we've played on the polished Siberian pine stages of concert halls AND on sticky carpets, and created music in a wide variety of styles, ranging from cinematic soundscapes to radio-ready alternative rock (though only on the more discerning networks!). We've also played in tents, marquees, nightclubs, a cinema, a cathedral, and in a sailing club. And between shows we once slept at a golf club. Further to the subject of gigging, my role in the band is to speak, not to play any instruments and certainly not to sing. There are many moving parts in an endeavour like ours, all taken care of by people who know what they are doing, and in my case that means delivering language into a microphone in a manner not dissimilar to the way I would read a poem. On the records I am credited with 'talking'.

As well as finding the whole LYR project a reenergising experience, I've also found it liberating. I often compose lyrics on days when poetry feels beyond me, as if working in this new territory has provided an unexpected release from the self-inflicted intensities of the day job, not least when I've been trying to out-stare a blank piece of paper or empty computer screen, hoping a poem will somehow surrender and reveal itself. With song lyrics I'm quite happy to blink first. Sometimes there isn't even a tune or arrangement waiting for the verses and choruses, and sometimes good intentions and enthusiastic agreements come to nothing, as the Miscellaneous section of this book confirms. If there's a third thing the music industry has taught me etc., etc. But that doesn't stop me composing, and these days I'm probably imagining Richard's falsetto in and among the words, or anticipating Patrick's piano chords beneath and above them. As pieces of text they are finished, but await transformation by music.

I wanted to publish this collection partly as a document of the work I've produced in this field, and partly because on more and more occasions I've been reciting song lyrics at my readings, as part of my, er, repertoire. On a practical level alone it's better to be reading from a book than juggling loose pages or trying to decipher scribbled handwriting. I'm not sure how they sound, out loud, *sans* music, because at the back of my mind I'm hearing melodies and time signatures and chord structures that aren't apparent to anyone else within earshot. But they seem to work, accompanied by an ensemble of silence.

Perhaps they have something that the poems don't. Or perhaps they don't have something that the poems do, a notion that I'm still processing.

Simon Armitage, 2023

# FELTHAM SINGS

# A Few Facts in Reverse Order

Ten – they peep through the spyhole, bang on the door.
Nine – I slept for a year on my cousin's floor.
Eight – you can lean on your mop for two hours a day.
Seven – only amnesia takes the past away.
Six – pin-stripe and denim are this year's black.
Five – the cops thought I'd been slashed by a wild cat.
Four – one man's life is another man's razor.
Three – they sent me away for skew-whiff behaviour.
Two – I once stole ice from the London marathon.
One – they watch me at night, I'm the night-watchman.

>*He once stole ice from the London marathon.*
>*We watch him at night, he's the night-watchman.*

Ten – I can bend a car door with my bare skin.
Nine – it takes exactly eleven minutes to swing.
Eight – you can't choose your family but you can choose your
   visitors.
Seven – I was manhandled once by babysitters.
Six – prison is a disease called boredom.
Five – I take snapshots of the cars I've stolen.
Four – one man's sheet is another man's rope.
Three – you can lose your footing on lino and soap.
Two – you can't overdose on two paracetamol.
One – they watch me at night, I'm the night-watchman.

>*He can't overdose on two paracetamol.*
>*We watch him at night, he's the night-watchman.*

Ten – my dad's waiting for his third heart attack.
Nine – my auntie's got six months to live, if that.

Eight – you wear your heart in your shirt pocket in this place.
Seven – a supper fit for a king is a Jaffa Cake.
Six – I'd never top myself, that's just madness.
Five – these cuts you see are from thorns and brambles.
Four – prison is the drip, drip, drip of a ping-pong ball.
Three – prison is the pip, pip, pip at the end of a phone call.
Two – your watch goes slow when it's clocking your lifespan.
One – they watch me at night, I'm the night-watchman.

*His watch goes slow when it's clocking his life-span.*
*We watch him at night, he's the night-watchman.*

# The Long Range Forecast

Some boy brushes your elbow and spills the drinks –
down comes the red mist.
Some boy offers a handshake that looks like a fist –
down comes the red mist.
Some boy thinks that he's so funny and so clever
but he's taking the piss.
High pressure. Stormy weather.
Down comes the red mist. DOWN COMES THE RED MIST.

This is the long-range forecast:
peacocks poncing around in the courtyard.

This is the long-range forecast:
two visits a month and four phone-cards.

This is the long-range forecast:
Now That's What I Call Mind-Numbing Boredom on all
    formats.

This is the long-range forecast:
peacocks bearing their arses before breakfast.

This is the long-range forecast:
two hundred boys in a marathon wank-fest.

This is the long-range forecast:
three hundred and sixty-five ways of eating a Mars Bar.

This is the long-range forecast:
two-fifty a week but no council tax.

This is the long-range forecast:
peacocks strutting about like bastards.

This is the long-range forecast:
car-crime nobodies versus the drug-running all-stars.

This is the long-range forecast:
a feast of Creme Eggs and Liquorice Allsorts.

This is the long-range forecast:
a future of pool cues and table tennis bats.

This is the long-range forecast:
peacocks bigging it up in the car-park.

This is the long-range forecast:
screws with clip-boards marking the scorecards.

This is the long-range forecast:
a windowsill full of family photographs.

This is the long-range forecast:
A peacock outside doing the royal walkabout.

This is the long-range forecast:
life burning away into smoke and fag-ash.

This is the long-rang forecast:
the sound of your own thoughts at full-blast.

This is the long-range forecast:
peacocks having it large on the flat roofs.

This is the long-range forecast
two visits a month and four phone-cards.

This is the long-range forecast:
down comes the red mist, put on your fog lamps.

# SONGBIRDS

# Down on Mary Street

Here comes the mufti squad to scissor off my clothes.
Here comes the goon squad with the stun-gun and the hose.
They'll put me in an arm-lock and they'll trigger back my
    thumb.
They'd pull my fingernails out but they're bitten to the stump.

Who me – I thought Tamazepam were little jelly sweets.
Who me – I thought Diazepam were after dinner treats.

Here comes scary Mary – someone hit the fire alarm.
She's cut her throat and slashed a barcode in her arm.
She went up in a ball of flames inside the padded cell –
but we were drinking tea and couldn't hear the panic bell.

Who me – I thought a prison was a fancy second home.
Who me – I thought a banquet was a bucket full of bones.

*And I'm oh so sorry that I spat my blood at you,*
*and I'm oh so oh so sorry that I split your head in two,*
*see I was fifteen when it happened and I didn't even bleed,*
*and I'm still down there,*
       *I'm still down there,*
           *I'm down on Mary Street.*

Here comes some punter in his swanky new car.
Here comes the Vaseline and the weight-lifting bar. . .

Who me – I thought a national park was a prison yard.
Who me – I thought a flick-knife was a cashpoint card.

*And I'm oh so sorry that I hissed at you,*
*and I'm oh so oh so sorry that I threw my piss at you,*
*see I was fifteen when it happened and I didn't even bleed,*
*and I'm still down there,*
>*I'm still down there,*
>>*I'm down on Mary Street.*

>>Hey mother, can't you see me.
>>Up on the balcony.
>>I'm waving at you mother as you stumble through
>>    the park.
>>I'm waving at you, mother, but you never wave back.

Don't give her back her life she won't know what to do.
Don't send her back outside she wouldn't have a clue.
Don't leave the door ajar she's better off inside
Don't say I said so BUT THEY'RE ABSOLUTELY RIGHT.

*And I'm oh so sorry that I trashed this place*
*and I'm oh so oh so sorry that I'm always in your face*
*see I was fifteen when it started and I didn't even bleed*
*and I'm still down there*
>*I'm still down there*
>>*I'm down on Mary Street.*

# Song of the Songbird

### (A Lullaby)

Sleep, little chick, through stormy weather,
mammy flew off and lost a feather,
but ever she's coming with corn in her beak,
so sleep, little songbird, sleep.

Sleep, little chick, through midnight dark,
the trap was set and mammy got caught
but never no trap will ever her keep
so sleep, little songbird, sleep.

Soon I'll be climbing into the sky,
sleep, little songbird, close your eyes,
yon hunting hawks won't never get me
sleep, little songbird, don't forget me . . .

Sleep, little songbird, mammy did wrong,
but ever she's calling, singing her song,
and ever you're dandled in mammy's nest,
under mammy's wing, under mammy's breast.

Sleep, little songbird, go to sleep,
you'll always be mammy's in mammy's dreams
sleep, little songbird, go to sleep,
sleep, little songbird, sleep . . .

Cardigan Girl

Cardigan girl on the unmanned station
trains haven't stopped here since the dawn of creation
I'm watching you now through the upstairs curtains
cardigan girl, cuur cardigan girl.

Cardigan girl with your retro stripes on
a bag where me could kill your reputation
but it's not in my nature to try and suggest some
shenanigans girl, cuu cardigan girl.

Have you really got somewhere better to go
like a Cardigans gig or a Charlatans show
are you feeling the heat in this most unEnglish weather?

If I came down there with melted snow
and some tunes I taped from a radio show
could we sit and drink and listen and talk together
                              until whenever...

Cardigan girl with your knitwear and jeans on
are you cold to the bones or is coolness the reason
your sweaters are white at the height of the season
ptarmigan girl, cuu cardigan girl

# Cardigan Girl

Cardigan girl on the unmanned station,
trains haven't stopped here since the dawn of creation,
I'm watching you now through the upstairs curtains,
cardigan girl, c-c-c-cardigan girl.

Cardigan girl with your retro shades on,
a boy like me could kill your reputation
but it's not in my nature to try and suggest some
shenanigans girl, c-c-c-cardigan girl.

*Have you really got somewhere better to go,*
*like a Cardigans gig or a Charlatans show,*
*are you feeling the heat in this most un-English weather?*

*If I came down there with melted snow*
*and some tunes I taped from a radio show*
*could we sit and drink and listen and talk together?*
*Until whenever?*

Cardigan with your knitwear and jeans on,
are you cold to the bones or is coolness the reason
your feathers are white at the height of the season,
ptarmigan girl, c-c-c-cardigan girl.

> Would you think me forward if I smiled or waved, girl?
> Would you think me backward if I opened my cakehole?
> Am I something stuck to the tap-room carpet,
> am I something left over at the farmer's market?

Cardigan girl on the empty platform,
I'm thinking of entering terminal free fall,

thinking of chucking myself at your feet, girl,
cardigan girl, c-c-c-cardigan girl.

Cardigan girl on the unmanned station,
trains haven't stopped here since the dawn of creation,
I'm watching you now through the upstairs curtains,
cardigan girl, c-c-c-cardigan girl.

# From the Shorelines of Venus

It's not true.
  Don't let them needle you.
      It's just the jealous few,
  doing what needles do.
And it's not true.

It's not true.
  Don't let them get to you.
      It's only one or two
  dying to turn the screw.
And it's not true.

At the height of the season
in a laughable blouse,
you came with a suitcase and laughed at my house.

Don't buy their deceiving,
when they blacken my name.
Don't give them a reason to leave me again.

It's not true.
  Don't let it eat at you.
      That way they've beaten you.
  I'd never cheat on you.
And it's not true.

It's not true.
  I was just passing there.
      This slender thread of hair
  could be from anywhere.
And it's not true.

From the shorelines of Venus
into Mercury's skies,
I swear on my grave they're unspeakable lies.

From the mouths of those creatures
comes nothing but bile,
they're halving and halving the worth of my soul.

It's born from the meanness,
of their own sorry lives,
they're nothing but poisonous,
whispering,
muck-raking,
back-biting,
mud-slinging,
side-winding come here to . . .

. . . mouth off their treasons,
and squeal from their sties,
and all that I've dreamed of now drowns in their lies.

They claim that they've seen me,
they've heard from their spies,
they're nothing but bad-mouthing,
supergrass,
ear-wigging,
tongue-wagging,
planting the Judas kiss come here to . . .

. . . blame me and bleed me
with leaches and lies,
and all that's between us now darkens and dies.

# Grouse Beaters Boys' Club

You're back from doing your degree
and all the regulars agree,
you're someone different.

We're in the snug room of the Swan,
you're talking Freud and going on
about some Russian dissident.

*Grouse Beaters Boys' Club cross your hearts and hope to die,*
*marching out of a bloodshot August sky.*

Your girlfriend's training as a vet,
she's smoking Gauloise cigarettes
and quoting T. S. Eliot.

She did her gap year in New York,
she simplifies things when we talk
like I'm the village idiot.

*Grouse Beaters Boys' Club cross your hearts and hope to die,*
*marching out of a bloodshot August sky.*

> Meanwhile in the studio,
> a legend discusses his tale of woe.
> He denies he's become a monster,
> he'll be back after these short words from his sponsor.

I haven't see you for a year
so it's a big surprise to hear
about your social conscience.

Whatever happened to the kid
who bragged that everything he did
was total nonsense.

    Meanwhile on the radio,
    the DJ's got some place else to go.
    Send a text if you're already missing him,
    but that's the end of the show, thanks for listening.

Grouse Beaters Boys' Club (Cross Your Hearts and Hope to Die)

You're back from doing your degree
and all the regulars agree
~~you ain't the lad that you were~~ ~~your thought complete~~
you're someone different

*you're the other*
*you're someone different*
*you've changed completely*
*what could I say*
*you're not the same now*

We're in the snug room of the Swan
you're spouting Freud and going on
about the ~~bigger ego, this theory~~ *but let dreams mean*
some Russian dissident

Grouse Beaters Boys Club cross your hearts and hope to die
coming out of a Woodshit August day.

Your girlfriend's training as a vet
she's smoking Gaulois cigarettes
and quoting T.S. Eliot.

She did her gap-year in New York
she simplifies behind when we talk
like I'm the village idiot.

Grouse Beaters Boys Club cross your hearts and hope to die
coming out of a Woodshit August day.

Meanwhile on the giant screen      *Meanwhile in the studio*
a legend discusses the price of fame      *a legend discusses his tale of woe*
he denies he's become a monster
he'll be back after these short words from his sponsor.....

23

# Legendary

The night surrendered meekly,
the dream began to fade,
the sun rose high
and bleached the dye
from every map you made.
The wind-up clock
you prayed had stopped
threw up its false alarm,
your hand dragged back the curtain
on a cold and queasy, slow uneasy calm.

Down among the accidents,
slushing through the snow,
at times you find the *Welcome* signs
are only there for show.
The neon lights
will all swear blind
you're just seconds now from fame.
You know they're out to bleed you
but you'll follow where they lead you
just the same.

*The smallest thing's the thing to fear,*
*your sister's in the bathtub fighting back the big tears.*
*The neighbours sigh*
*as you sidle by,*
*they'd kill you if they thought that you were half alive.*
*The kettle's on*
*but the dream's long gone,*
*you'll drive your mother's car into history –*
*you don't know what you will be but you will be legendary.*

Confusion at the superstore,
the system melting down,
refusal at the hurdle
of the cheapest drink in town.
The tearful part-time checkout girl
gets threatened with the sack.
Overcome with compassion,
you take the booze
out of the basket
and put it back.

Blizzards sweep the precinct,
twilight swipes the streets,
some well-known lass
now cast in brass
stands shaky on her feet.
Her eyes look south
her frozen mouth
speaks words both loud and true:
she says anywhere but here, kid,
and everyone and anyone but you.

# Tea Leaves

I think the tea leaves could be right, I think it's going to be
    fantastic,
fishing silver from the drains,
riding shotgun on the trains.
The cash-flow situation's tight but we can shove it all on plastic,
scooping honey from the trees,
pulling money from the breeze.

*And what you want of me*
    *and what I want of you*
        *are just the same.*
*It doesn't matter*
    *that in seven weeks*
        *I've never asked your name.*
*Down beneath the blankets*
    *where the treasure's buried*
        *we'll be millionaires.*
*Don't touch the light-switch*
    *or the bubble bursts*
        *and leaves us in mid-air.*

There was someone else it's true, but it never even felt right.
It was always on the rocks
since she changed the locks.
Yeah that's her on this tattoo, but it isn't even spelt right.
Never dabble with the Quink
after drowning in the drink.

*And what you want of me . . .*

Nothing ventured nothing gained,
let your hair down for a change,
we'll have everything and more
what are you waiting for?

We'll take whatever we can get,
double cream from every step,
I'll do all the literature,
practising your signature,
yellow bricks will line the way,
all aboard the gravy train,
it's a better man that gets it all for free.

You can do the maths,
this way down the primrose path,
iron gates will open wide,
bodyguards will step aside,
clever clogs will run away,
lazy bones will turn to clay,
it's a bitter man who pins the blame on me.

# I AM THOMAS

# Aikenhead's Telescope

*Roll up, roll up, come see the light,*
*let the glow of the universe enter the mind.*

Look hard at the moon, see it close and clear.
What looms in the glass is no heavenly sphere
or celestial circle, perfectly formed,
but a lump of geology, pockmarked and flawed.

*Roll up, roll up, come see the light,*
*let the glow of the universe enter the mind.*

If there's no divine architect, think what it means:
space is a country of infinite dreams,
an endless range of uncountable stars
and worlds spinning round them, worlds like ours.

> Not a here and now, not the life we're in,
> where fear and frost get under the skin
> and taxes ripen as crops grow thin
> and caps are doffed to foreign crowns
> and kindness sours and hunger growls
> and a storm from the pulpit blasts and howls . . .

*Roll up, roll up, come see the light,*
*let the glow of the universe enter the mind.*

If you stare for long enough into the dark
you'll start seeing faces, eyes looking back:
their earth in our telescopes, ours in theirs,
and nothing between us but miles and years.

*Roll up, roll up, come see the light,*
*let the glow of the universe enter the mind.*

Call me an infidel, call me a fool,
I believe some day we'll fly to the moon,
build a shimmering city from silver stones,
worship the sun as it feeds our bones.

> Not a here and now, not the life we're in,
> where fear and frost get under the skin
> and taxes ripen as crops grow thin
> and caps are doffed to foreign crowns
> and kindness sours and hunger growls
> and a storm from the pulpit blasts and howls . . .

There's far more wonder in this device
than a holy book could ever describe;
lean into the lens and believe your eyes,
there's no heaven up there, just astonishing skies.

The cosmos is waiting, vast and bright,
the door of the future stands open wide,
there are planets and people, beyond the black,
it's no miracle, though, it's better than that.

It's greater and grander and finer and further
and bigger and braver and better than that.

*Roll up, roll up, come see the light,*
*let the glow of the universe enter the mind.*

# Nativity Song

Cold sounds the bell
outside these walls.
The flock beds down,
a barn owl calls.
Sharp lies the frost
like glassy thorns.
Tight grows the wood
that bears the nails.

Soft falls the snow
beyond these bars.
Three magi chart
a risen star.
The white lamb kneels
with ass and ox.
Stiff stands the tree
that shapes the cross.

Deep drift the flakes
in wynds and lanes.
The moon peers in
with a mother's face.
The Christ-child sleeps
in his makeshift crib.
Firm holds the branch
that forms the jib.

Clean cuts the breeze
over lochs and glens.
Far reach the roots
of tongues of men.

The bull stands mute
with goat and horse.
Tight twists the noose
of godless thoughts.

Slow burns the wick
in the lantern's eye.
A manger kindles
innocent life.
Faint glows the fire
of coming day
to welcome those
who wake to die.

Of coming day.
Who wake to die.

# Parable

All the seed wanted to do was sow.
And all the wheat wanted to do was grow.
And all the farmer wanted to do was reap.
But all the cat wanted to do was sleep.
And all the dog wanted to do was snore.
And all the rat wanted to do was gorge,
munch at the stalk, steal from the store.

Then all the sparrows wanted a bite.
Then all the pigeons wanted a slice.
Then all the field mice wanted a piece.
Then all the locusts wanted a feast.
Then all the rooks wanted a go.
Then all the crows wanted to do was crow.

Then all the wife wanted to do was weep.
Then all the children went pale and sick.
Then every coin under the pillow was spent.
Then all the crops in the field went bad.
Then the lamp grew dark and the fire grew cold.
And the flock – the flock wandered far from the fold.

See, the problem had to be nipped in the bud.
See, the rot had to be ripped out down to the root.
So the rat was trapped, snared by its foot,
hung on a fence with a barb through its nose.
Then all the rooks and sparrows and pigeons and crows
took off for the hills, and lived among stones.
Then all the seed had to do was sow.
Then all the wheat had to do was grow.

*And you're the farmer – is that what you're saying?*

No, I'm the rat-catcher. Start praying.

# The Drunken Friends

After you, sir.
    *You're a true sir.*
Be my guest, sir.
    *You're the best, sir.*
What are friends for?

      Any reason,
      any season,
      I'll be there for
      you I swear, sir.

Take the best chair
by the hearth, sir.
    *Have my Scotch broth.*
    *Get the lot scoffed.*
What are friends for?

      Arm in arm and
      blood to blood, squire,
      you're the kind I'd
      walk through fire for.

Shake my hand, kid.
    *Put it there, bud.*
Come to me lets
have a man-hug.
    *What are friends for?*

We are one, what's
mine is yours, if
someone hurts you
they hurt me too.

Drink my last dram.
    *You're a gent, lad.*
It's true love, man.
    *Steady on, son.*
What are friends for?

    S'getting late, you
    have my bed, the
    sheets are clean, mate.
    Just to sleep, right?

Take my purse since
you're the poorer.
    *Are you sure, sir?*
Never surer.
    *What are friends for?*

    Any crime or
    any secret,
    blurt it out I
    shan't repeat it.

Brother, soul-mate,
you're the type that
I'd put my neck
on the line for.

*Speak my mind for.*
Or do time or
do or die for.
    *What are friends for?*

    You're the bestest.
    Thick as thieves, us.
    Tried and tested.
    True and trusted.

Here's to you, chum.
    *Here's to you, Tom.*
Best of friends, sir.
    *Till the end, sir.*
What are friends for?

# 33 1/3

They forced the door
    and found in the bed-sit
        the pulsing hook-line

of diamond on vinyl,
    the arm still ploughing
        the run-out spiral,

the lost module
    of cartridge and stylus
        in captured orbit

around the spindle, a looped,
    circling, whirlpooling swansong
        that died as they craned up

the weightless needle
    and lowered him down
        on the rope that he swung from.

# Adam's Apple

He soaks in the bath till his skin
    softens and floats,
takes a blade to his chin,
    gets close.

Under a white shirt
    he's gone thin.
You could hang coats on his breastbone,
    play tunes on his ribs.

He pulls on a black suit,
    buffs up his boots with spit.
His gums weep – traces of tears
    leave pink stripes in the sink.

He handles the black tie, charms it
    into a loose knot;
the man in the mirror
    eases it up to his throat.

Stood in the doorway
    he watches her . . . sees her
play God with her hair,
    bring gold to her neck.

The taste and stink
    of powders and scents
go far back
    into a deep hole. *Let go.*

*Let go. Let go. Let go.*

He pulls on the black suit,
    the boots polished with spit.
Then hoists it into the flesh,
    the black tie

he's been hanging onto,
    holding back for this.

# Greatcoat

Stands up on its own when you're not around,
smells like a dog, smells like it drowned,
and the arm that plucked the buttercup
still throws a decent uppercut.

What have you got in your pockets there?
A fingernail and a hank of hair.
Twenty quid and a rolled up dollar.
A soft toy choked in a pit bull's collar.

> *It's a greatcoat, feller,*
> *climbing the stairs from the locked up cellar.*
> *It's a great coat all right, now that you're gone.*
> *Just never ask me to put it on.*

Lined with satin, hem to cuff,
the iron fist and the velvet glove.
Turning your shadow into a coat
was darkness embodied, a masterstroke.

Here's the avenue, here's the address,
windows boarded, garden's a mess,
here's the gibbet, the peg on the door
where the greatcoat hangs right down to the floor.

> Under its weight you're buried alive,
> under its wing the raven flies.
> But I'm ditching you, brother, dropping you off
> on the piss-stained steps of the charity shop.

It's a great coat, your worship,
looms like a zeppelin, glides like a warship.

*It's a greatcoat, feller,*
*climbing the stairs from the locked up cellar.*
*It's a great coat all right, now that you're gone.*
*Just never ask me to put it on.*

# Leaves on the Line

In the past he was coming by steam and coal,
by breath of water and flame of stone.
We waited for hours then buggered off home;

>   till Leaf Man come
>   how long, how long?

At present he comes by diesel and spark,
with an ear to the rail we can hear him talk.
We wait all day then die in the dark;

>   how sung, how sung
>   the Leaf Man song?

Tomorrow he'll come on a beam of light,
rise like morning, end this wait.
But the rooster crowed and he's already late;

>   till Leaf Man come, how long, how long,
>   how sung, how sung the Leaf Man song?

# Never Good with Horses

You were happiest in the darkroom
conjuring shadows and shades,
running film through your dry fingers,
keeping ghosts in their graves.

And you could handle a steering wheel,
rounding the corners and bends,
watching the movie of life play out
through the windscreen's lens.

*But you were never good with horses,*
        *were you, my dear?*
*Always took a step backwards*
        *when they came near.*
*Couldn't bear to look in the dark rock pools*
        *of their eyes.*
*Couldn't hold your hand flat and offer*
        *your sugar cube lies.*

Thanks for the dried buttercups
pressed between faded pages,
thanks for the tropical butterflies
pinned in their glass cases.

For the snow-white rabbit's foot
screwed to a key fob, all of my thanks,
and the skull studded with precious stones
and sharks in their glass tanks.

*But you were never good with horses,*
        *were you, my dear.*

*Always took a step backwards*
    *when they came near.*
*Couldn't bear to look in the dark rock pools*
    *of their eyes.*
*Couldn't hold your hand flat and offer*
    *your sugar cube lies.*

You said a man with his own telescope
isn't especially strange,
and to be a collector of doll's houses
is fine for a guy of your age.

I said look at their pretty ankles
and smooth coats, look at the grey and the black,
but you wanted the painted, wooden kind
you could rock this way and that.

*And you were never good with horses,*
    *were you, my dear?*
*Always took a step backwards*
    *when they came near.*
*Couldn't bear to look in the dark rock pools*
    *of their eyes.*
*Couldn't hold your hand flat and offer*
    *your sugar cube lies.*

# Product Testing

On.
Off.
On.
Off.
On.
Off.
On.
Off.
On.
Off.
On.
Off.
Yep, seems to work.

# The First Time

Your boyfriend of choice was older than me,
his slip-ons were parked underneath the settee.
I'd got no right to be making a call
but I walked home next morning eleven feet tall.

We were torturing stories, dissecting a scene
from *The Power and the Glory* by Graham Greene.
'Shall we cut to the chase?' – that's what you said
with your mother barely asleep overhead.

    *Call it the first time,*
*call it the last time,*
*call me a dead guy,*
    *for dredging up past times,*

    *gone your own way now,*
*nothing to say now,*
*still mouthing your name, though,*
    *ten years to the day now.*

Did you marry that chump with the fags and the cash
and the clapped-out Ford and the copper's moustache?
Did he ever twig that a bare-faced boy
had stolen at dusk through the gates of Troy?

I found some hair and some bubble-gum
and a telephone number that plays it dumb,
and the beautifully filthy word that you wrote
in purple ink on a post-it note: FUCK?

*Call it the first time,*
*call it the last time,*
*call me a dead beat,*
      *for slicing up dead meat,*

      *gone your own way now,*
*nothing to say now,*
*still mouthing your name, though,*
      *ten years to the day now.*

# The National Trust Range of Paints Colour Card

String and Pigeon and Sugar Bag Light,
Lichen and Powder Blue.
>    *I can sing a rainbow, sing a rainbow,*
>    *sing a rainbow too.*

Hay and Biscuit and Hardwick White,
Buff and Berrington Blue.
>    *Poverty's a shame though, is a shame though,*
>    *is a shame it's true.*

Drab and Olive and Buff and Bone,
Down Pipe and Ballroom Blue.
>    *Nobody's to blame though, is to blame though,*
>    *is to blame but you.*

Eating Room Red and London Stone,
Fowler Pink, Cane and Hague Blue.
>    *I can see the grain grow, see the grain grow,*
>    *see the grain grow through.*

# Urban Myth #91

Mr lorry driver, drop me off,
I've heard your gears grinding for long enough.
You can stuff your call signs and your citizen's band,
your greasy sex in the back of the cab,
you can keep your oily mind and diesel knuckles
on your confederate belt-buckle.
Indicate and pull over,
just here on the hard shoulder.

> *Urban Myth #91:*
> *Central Reservation Man.*
> *Tramping Britain's middle lane*
> *between the triple carriageways.*
> *Tightrope-walking the thin line*
> *between the barricades.*

Mr sales representative let me cross
to that untrodden groove of litter and wild grass.
There's a life to be lived on that narrow strip,
sucking the juice from lollipop sticks,
smoking the dying breath of cigarette dimps.
I'm going to bed down at night with the wounded badgers
under the concrete bridges.

> *Urban Myth #91:*
> *Central Reservation Man.*
> *Tramping Britain's middle lane*
> *between the triple carriageways.*
> *Tightrope-walking the thin line*
> *between the barricades.*

Mr officer-of-the-law leave me to it.
I'm not jay-walking, I'm not exceeding the speed limit.
Do I cause offence to the traffic cop
in my crisp-packet gloves and styrofoam cap,
with my dandelion-clock candy floss,
with my precious beads of windscreen glass?
Put a sock in the siren, lieutenant.
Tea-cosy the blue-light, sergeant.

> *Urban Myth #91:*
> *Central Reservation Man.*
> *Tramping Britain's middle lane*
> *between the triple carriageways.*
> *Tightrope-walking the thin line*
> *between the barricades.*

Mr closed-circuit television operator
I've seen the inner workings of beautiful creatures:
dogs peering out of Christmas crackers,
a human heart rolled in tissue paper,
an Alsatian puppy still in its wrapper.
There are things a camera doesn't pick up
down here in the stitchwort and elderflower.
So zoom out. Blindfold the aperture.

> *Urban Myth #91:*
> *Central Reservation Man.*
> *Tramping Britain's middle lane*
> *between the triple carriageways.*
> *Tightrope-walking the thin line*
> *between the barricades.*

# Zodiac T-Shirt

The avenues marching
with combat shorts,
the pavements strutting
with micro-skirts.

No rest from the sun,
a smothering heat
like a mother beast
asleep on its young.

> *Zodiac T-shirt,*
> *paper-clip bracelet,*
> *mercury rising,*
> *call in the crash-team.*

Knock for knock
and tit for tat,
your bike got nicked
so you nicked one back.

We pull up a tree
and plant a rose,
where a cigarette dies,
another one grows.

> *Zodiac T-shirt,*
> *paper-clip bracelet,*
> *mercury rising,*
> *call in the crash-team.*

Hand in hand
when the bend-i-bus stopped,
a couple got on,
a couple got off,

and an ice-cream wept
on the steps of the church
and the crusted-up reservoir
died of thirst.

>Zodiac T-shirt,
>paper-clip bracelet,
>mercury rising,
>call in the crash-team.

Drink for drink
in the park that night,
me scratching yours
you scratching mine,

till the words came thumping
hand over fist,
and the sky blew a fuse
and it started to piss

>on your Zodiac T-shirt,
>paper-clip bracelet,
>crucifix pendant,
>cinnamon toothpaste,
>chewing-gum pavement,
>liquorice protest,
>dragonfly heartbeat,
>daisy-chain necklace,
>candy-stripe shoelace,
>fingerbob Jesus,

*pregnancy dipstick,*
*all back to your place,*
*body-bag suitcase,*
*mercury rising,*
*cardiac jump-leads,*
*call in the crash-team, call in the crash-team,*
*call in the crash-team, call in the crash-team.*

## Candles & Blue Cake

Let's drive to the reservoir,
the one with the drowned church,
watch cars streaming under our feet
from the shivering bridge.

*I kept the receipt,*
*candles & blue cake.*

The full moon's an usherette
showing us to our seats;
to me a meteorite shower
is a well-chosen gift.

*I kept the receipt,*
*candles & blue cake.*

I spent a fortune on tomorrow –
peel off the wrapping of night.
The stars are cigarette burns
in the fancy raincoat you hate.

*I kept the receipt,*
*candles & blue cake.*

# Cascade Theory

The world fragmented, I got things wrong,
played a furloughed god in the Church of None,
'ran the clock down' as the pundits say,
dropped a toy boat in next door's pond
and called it a song, broke a borrowed scythe
on a hidden rock mowing wet hay. Hey, hey!

*Space junk, colliding with space junk,*
*upsetting the top saints.*
*And all it takes is a fleck of paint . . .*

'Look who it isn't,' someone snarked
in Millennium Square. It was market day –
loaves and cakes like defused mines.
They built a business park in a green field
while I fiddled about and fine-tuned
the useless haiku of a Rubik's cube.

*Space junk, colliding with space junk,*
*upsetting the top saints.*
*And all it takes is a fleck of paint . . .*

But stone the crows we've come a long way,
counting the cats' eyes, driving on fumes,
pilfering coins from roadside shrines.
Captain's Log: satellite sex with Mission Control.
OK if I make the tears happen now, old man?
In the face of Jesus I saw the orangutan.

*Space junk, colliding with space junk,*
*upsetting the top saints.*
*And all it takes is a fleck of paint . . .*

# Country Club

From the flushed cheeks of the powdered women
and their cockeyed men, it entered my head
they'd all been screwing while dressing for dinner.
Every room had a wall-mounted sink
and a mottled and mildewed hunting scene.
The widowed baroness sat on her isms
like a dodo hatching a Fabergé egg;
under the table many hands went AWOL.
To wash down the snotty oysters I swigged
the lemony scent in the fingerbowl;
a string quartet sawed through 'I Am the Walrus'.
Some retired to the billiard room
or took to the terrace for coffee and cognac.
Others smoked skunk in the swimming pool:
pinned hairdos and strapless shoulders floated
on lily pads of silken ball-gowns;
gentlemen in white shirts and black tailcoats
were killer whales crossed with deformed tadpoles.

Your little pinkie hovered over the shrimp fork
then counterbalanced a gilded tea-cup.

# Lockdown

And I couldn't escape the waking dream
of infected fleas

in the warp and weft of soggy cloth
by the tailor's hearth

in ye olde Eyam.
Then couldn't un-see

the Boundary Stone,
that cock-eyed dice with its six dark holes,

thimbles brimming with vinegar wine
purging the plagued coins.

Which brought to mind the sorry story
of Emmott Syddall and Rowland Torre,

star-crossed lovers on either side
of the quarantine line

whose wordless courtship spanned the river
*till she came no longer.*

But slept again,
and dreamt this time

of the exiled *yaksha* sending word
to his lost wife on a passing cloud,

a cloud that followed an earthly map
of camel trails and cattle tracks,

streams like necklaces,
fan-tailed peacocks, painted elephants,

embroidered bedspreads
of meadows and hedges,

bamboo forests and snow-hatted peaks,
waterfalls, creeks,

the hieroglyphs of wide-winged cranes
and the glistening lotus flower after rain,

the air
hypnotically see-through, rare,

the journey a ponderous one at times, long and slow
but necessarily so.

Lockdown

And I couldn't escape the whining stream
of infected fleas

in the warp and weft of ragged cloth
of the killer's heart that [...]

in ye olde Eyam.
Their costive gunsee

the Boundary Stone
that cock-eyed sieve with its six data holes.

thimbles brimmed with vinegar wine
purging the plagued coins.

Which brought to mind the sorry story
of Emmott Sydall and Rowland Torre.

star-crossed lovers on either side
of the quarantine line

those worthless earthling spurned the river
till she came no longer.

But slept again
and dreamt this time

of the exiled [...] sending word
to his lost wife on a passing cloud.

a cloud that billowed on earthly [...]
of vapour trails and little trains,

steam [...] near fishes,
[...] penguins, painted elephants.

# Luna Maria

So how's the sea?
   It didn't rain there?
      It rained here.

I'll make do
   with the sky for now;
      open the window,

put the moon in your eye.
   It rained there, didn't it?
      It didn't rain here.

*Luna maria*, oceans and lakes
   on the moon's face,
      some named

after states of mind.
   It didn't rain here.
      Did it rain there?

Are you waving?
   Go to the shoreline
      and wait, I'm wading

though deep air.
   Didn't it rain there?
      It rained here.

# Omen

I found a dirk,
buried point first
in garden dirt,

sunk like a curse
or left as a wish
in deep earth.

*What's a dirk?*
*Only a knife that can see in the dark.*

Laid in the hand:
the equipoise
of handle and blade,

the hope and guilt
of a bone haft
and a stone hilt.

*What's a dirk?*
*Only a knife that can see in the dark.*

Stab the earth
        to puncture a lung
                or pierce a heart:

was bad blood
        the meaning of this,
                or was it love?

Let the record say love.

*What's a dirk?*
*Only a knife that can see in the dark.*

# Redwings

The oak the oak,
in his new green coat,
such soul and heart

and the last to moult,
but all you were after
was timber and smoke.

So it's true, the redwings are here again.
Dusk and dawn tucked under their wings.
O Stockholm with your iron trees.
We must not say what the redwings mean.

The ash the ash,
she was handing you
the keys to the house,

she was praying you'd pop
the question at last,
but you never asked.

So it's true, the redwings are here again.
Dusk and dawn tucked under their wings.
O Oslo with your iron trees.
We must not say what the redwings mean.

The beech the beech,
in his fingerless gloves
and mossy green sleeves,

if he begs for love
will you make him crawl
on his hands and knees?

The lime the lime,
she's worn her hair
the way you like,

she's come to the rave
in her favourite dress
and you couldn't care less.

So it's true, the redwings are here again.
Dusk and dawn tucked under their wings.
O Saltholm frozen in iron seas.
We must not say what the redwings mean.

So it's true, the redwings are here again.
Embers pocketed under their wings.
Poor chandeliers of evergreens.
Poor redwings caught in the iron breeze.
We must not say what the redwings mean.

# Winter Solstice

It's cold in the small hours, bolting the door against
dark nights,
scanning for miracles, panning for glimmers
and signs,
knowing at best I'm the tenth or eleventh
in line.
I know I'm not really your favourite person
but you're mine.

(*'Desire as a sylph-figured creature who changes
her mind'*)

This is the view, here's how it looks from
the side lines,
clutching at straws, reaching for shadows
and lifelines,
dredging the shallows for proof and clues
in the half-light.
This is the news, this is me living
the half-life.

I heard you'd been dishing the dirt that I'm selfless
and kind,
more like a brother or sister, not really
your type,
then later I whisper, 'I need to be worshipped
not just liked.'
I know I'm not really your favourite person
but you're mine.

Cut to the part where snowdrop revels
in sunlight,
spare me the sympathy card with its chorus
of dumb rhymes,
tear me apart with the love-heart declaring
LOVE IS BLIND.
I know I'm not nearly your favourite person
but you're mine.

I know I'm not really your favourite person
but you're mine.

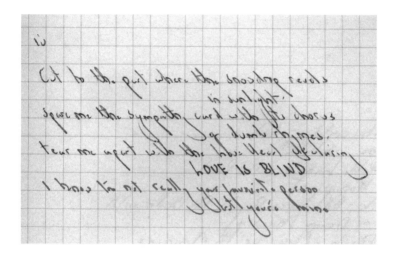

# WE'LL SING

# The Song Thrush and the Mountain Ash

Through the hospital window
    she said to me
she'd forgotten the name
    of her special tree,
and forgotten the name
    of her favourite bird.
Through the hospital window
    I mouthed the words:

the song thrush and the mountain ash.

Through the hospital window
    she asked again
why I stood outside
    in the wind and rain,
and said she didn't
    understand
why I didn't want
    to touch her hand.

The song thrush and the mountain ash.

She said she liked
    the flowers I sent
but wondered why
    they had no scent,
and why the food
    had lost its taste,
and why the nurse
    had covered her face?

And why the gates of the park were shut?
And why the shops were boarded up?
And why the swings were tied in knots?
And the music . . . why had the music stopped?

Through the hospital window
    I called her name
and waited a while
    but she never came,
then I saw reflected
    in the glass
the song thrush
    and the mountain ash.

The song thrush and the mountain ash.

# We'll Sing

A train in the sidings aches with rust,
the motorway makes an emergency stop,
a single vapour trail drifts and melts,
Wilson has swapped his pipe for a mask.

*Till the world discovers its voice again*
*we'll sing, we'll sing.*

The shopping centres are overgrown,
it's always Sunday, except in church,
a traffic light runs through its range of moves
but nobody stops and nobody goes.

*Till the world discovers its voice again*
*we'll sing, we'll sing.*

A downpour drums on the bandstand roof,
the west wind strums the trees in the copse,
sunlight fingers the cobweb harps,
a blackbird stirs and opens its throat.

*Till the world discovers its voice again*
*we'll sing, we'll sing.*

# FIRM AS A ROCK WE STAND

FIRM AS A ROCK WE STAND

# Addison Drifts

Some say she left in winter,
tiptoed through snow trailing black splinters
of coal, her name traced in frost
on a brick wall with a gloved finger.

Some say she left on her own,
no goodbyes, set off with a stone
in her shoe and an anthracite heart
down the turnpike road, alone.

Some say she left in the dark,
a midnight flit under the black arch
of the sky, the wick turned down
and warm ash in the hearth.

Above
    the spinal fluid of the Tyne,
    the fire escape of the Haltwhistle line;

Among
    the fidgety crows and gossipy trees,
    the ghostly footfall of autumn leaves.

Some say she visits now and again,
carves Addison, ADDISON into the grain
of goat willow, holly or silver birch;
washes her hair in the rain.

# Alchemy

Into the fire went copper.
And into the fire went zinc.
And into the fire went hunger.
And into the fire went coal.
And into the fire went weather.
And into the fire went steam.
And into the fire went marrow.
And into the fire went work.
And into the fire went dragons.
And into the fire went sleep.
And into the fire went atoms.
And into the fire went coins.
And into the fire went muscle.
And into the fire went rags.
And into the fire went sirens.
And out of the fire came . . . brass.

Then out of the brass came wonder.
And out of the brass came worth.
And out of the brass came marriage.
And out of the brass came bread.
And out of the brass came lions.
And out of the brass came sex.
And out of the brass came honey.
And out of the brass came shine.
And out of the brass came planets.
And out of the brass came dreams.
And out of the brass came medals.
And out of the brass came booze.
And out of the brass came banners.
And out of the brass came spires.

And out of the brass came pharaohs.
And out of the brass came fire.

Out of the earth came light.
Out of the earth came breath.

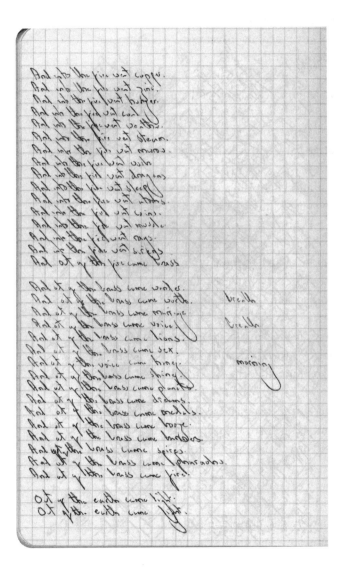

# Marsden by the Sea

In a force eight gale the lighthouse twizzles
like a barber's pole. On the upper deck
the jewelled lantern floats and meditates
in a quicksilver bed; its insect eye
looks sideways at the field in the field.

This dandelion clock was an oil lamp, once.

Oystercatchers trumpet the ghostly notes
of the prize band with their orange kazoos.

Clifftop allotments yield a summer crop
of pollen spores; in winter it's hailstones.

*Firm As a Rock We Stand* the banner sings,
but a limestone arch thrown up in the year dot
collapsed in pity after the last door
was slammed shut – a marooned stack now sulks.

The gates stayed open after the school closed;
the North Sea was the last lesson. Please note
the horizon pinned to the classroom wall.

Time's bulldozer trundles back and forth
but the mind's a kittiwake riding the air,
homing in on an old nesting site.

So memory crystallises into magnetite.

Sea-going terraces, built then scuttled
in the same bay. And on first name terms

with the streets: meet Charles, Henry,
William, Arthur, John and James – there's even
a Hilton, but no room service, no en suite.

The wind plays its concertina requiem.
The foghorn sympathises with the blue whale.

It's dark between pulses, though every five seconds
a red light catches shipwrecked villagers
playing sleeping tigers under the great lens.

# BARNSLEY –
## AN UNNATURAL HISTORY

# A Quiet Night Out with the Clowns

Forget the stag-party-circus-act vibe,
we're just homo sapiens' long lost tribe,
strolling the planet in spangly socks
and twirly bow-ties and stripy tops.

We're no street artists, just harmless old boys
whose fat shoes squeak like toddlers' toys
when we waddle home in November rain.
We talk about buses, talk about trains.

    *Seriously,*
*it's only a night out with the clowns.*
*No monkey business, no fooling around.*
*It's only a shuffling gaggle of innocent blokes*
*with scarlet wigs and some tired old jokes.*
*Just a quiet night out on the town with the clowns,*
*the moon coming up, the sun going down.*

And we never did no one or nothing no harm,
leap-frogging bollards, slaloming parked cars;
Weatherspoons, Ladbrokes, a pint and a flutter,
a fried chicken thigh and a piss in the gutter;

and things can turn sour in the indigo hours
but I never intended to squirt that flower
in the young Olympian's pale blue eye,
and no one got blinded, nobody died.

    *Trust me,*
*it's only a night out with the clowns.*
*No monkey business, no fooling around.*

It's only a shuffling gaggle of innocent blokes
with scarlet wigs and some tired old jokes.
Just a quiet night out on the town with the clowns,
the moon coming up, the sun going down.

Like a walking bus of glittery punks,
like elephants lumbering tail to trunk,
and I once got close to a friend who flinched
when mi day-glow lippy went all skewwhiff;

who might have followed me back to the house
but mi red cheeks smudged on her new cotton blouse
and she turned to stone when I said, 'If you like
you can perch on the front of mi one-wheel bike'.

As for this little man, a one-night stand
is a forty-watt bulb coming on in the hand,
And love is . . . conjuring turtledoves
from out of nowhere in polka-dot gloves.

Or it's home alone
with mi funny bone . . .

Honestly,
it's only a night out with the clowns.
No monkey business, no fooling around.
It's only a shuffling gaggle of innocent blokes
with scarlet wigs and some tired old jokes.
Just a quiet night out on the town with the clowns,
the moon coming up, the sun going down.

It's just Chucky and Bob, Binky and Bozo,
Ronald, the Joker, Pierrot and Coco,
harlequin cavemen,
hopscotching the pavement.

# After the Carnival

Outside the arcade
    the slipstream shuffles its feet
as the day heads west.

Behind the parade
    the sunset totters down Eldon Street
trailing its wedding dress.

*After the stilt-walkers – the litter pickers.*
*And a century flickers.*
*After the drum-majorettes – the street cleaners.*
*And the distance between us.*

A hi-viz jacket
    hauls in furlongs of bunting,
rounds up the traffic cones.

A spent rocket.
    Griffins scavenge the bins hunting
for phoenix bones.

*After the stilt-walkers – the litter pickers.*
*And a century flickers.*
*After the drum-majorettes – the street cleaners.*
*And the distance between us.*

I was a slow coach.
I dillied and dallied
behind the last float.
It was my own fault.

I shillied and shallied
till I missed the boat.

*After the stilt-walkers – the litter pickers.*
*And a century flickers.*
*After the drum-majorettes – the street cleaners.*
*And the distance between us.*

And the twilight thickens.
And the slowness . . . quickens.

An urban fox jinks
        though the mirrored Interchange
flaunting a burning cloak.

Ghosts finish their drinks
        in the Magnet Hotel and the Three Cranes
and the Royal Oak.

Starlings bisect the scene,
        car headlights rummage and root
in search of proof.

But what does it mean:
        a knee-length snakeskin boot
on a car roof.

Balloons in the nettles.
        Dusk waltzes across the border
twirling its bridal veil.

The glitter settles.
        Twilight glances over its shoulder
with its honeymoon smile.

Notes Towards A Song Called After The Parade

After the parade
a long day calls the street
tonite ......... weekly dress

Outside the arcade
the evening draws in to put
through the ......... times...

A ...... the socks done
on the ...... of a car

Standing along with the little girls

the prizes from the lost float —

confetti — purple and pink bows
would kill for you ...

Dealing the building in
......... the gutter down /town

The houses still warm

Come in                and left with the door open

And through the triumphal arch

a million caught on a flagpole
over the town hall ...

Marching band
take stage
drum majorettes
still within
..........
popcorn stalls

lifting their tongues soars
synth hits

........... the mind genies

missed the last

mustards in high vis
            ......

After the still-within ... the little girls
After the drum majorettes ...... the silent avenues

99

And the tremors elapse.
And the circus elopes

in its kitten heels
its deerstalker
its herringbone jumper
its dog collar

in its camel Crombie
its duck's arse
its leopard print dress
its moleskin kecks

in its beehive hair
its oxblood docs
its beetle crushers
its fishtail parka

in its donkey jacket
its whalebone corset
its Puma trainers
its turtleneck sweater

driving its Nissan Bluebird
its Volkswagen Beetle
its Chevy Cobra
its Alfa Spyder

driving its Mazda Bongo
its Mitsubishi Dingo
its Plymouth Barracuda
its Plymouth Road Runner

driving its Datsun Honey Bee
its Ford Mustang

its Ford Cougar
its Ford Bronco

driving its Dodge Viper
its Triumph Stag
its Chevy Impala
its Fiat Panda

# Fox on Eldon Street

She's crawled from under a glass-blower's moon,
the outermost tips of her fiber-optic fur
all blaze and flare, torched by streetlight.

She thinks:
*For chilblains apply iodine with a camelhair brush.*

She's collecting the metadata of stench
and stink – reefer butt, slippage of milkshake.
She's an instant hit of urban animalness
in the stagnant fishbowl of CCTV.

She thinks:
*Remove grease with blotting paper and a hot iron.*

She sees with her nose: the muzzle scopes
for the aphrodisiac of abandoned meat.

She thinks:
*Ripe tomatoes disperse ink from white cloth.*

She's eaten the embers of winter, she's eaten
cobwebs and pigeon feathers and smoke.

She thinks:
*Candle and salt make rusty iron as smooth as glass.*

She thinks:
*A ham should be soaked in tepid water overnight.*

Her shadow slopes off up the hollow arcade
to grub for jewels, re-joins her step for step
in the long low windows of Age Concern.

She thinks:
*Lavender oil stops flies landing on chandeliers.*

Under her paws the pavement's a sprung mattress.

She thinks:
*Hiccups are cured by sugar lumps soaked in vinegar wine.*

In the shantytown of allotments she caches
the day's shoplifting. Upside-down in the soil
a wheelbarrow mopes like a giant tortoise.

She thinks:
*Waterproof old boots with beeswax and mutton suet.*

A thousand tons of train clatters the iron bridge;
she beds down in the lair of her curled tail,
licks her cubs into life from lumps of coal.

# Hebrew Character

What are you doing here,
hunched in the widow frame
of this defunct phone box?
Was it the cold flame

of fluorescent light
that brought you rowing
over purple loosestrife,
buckthorn and rowan

into the concrete precinct?
I wouldn't dare touch
the fragile pencil shaving
of fur and rust, the magic dust

coating the drawn shields
of the wings, the pale stigmata
and endpaper foxing,
the smokescreen mantle.

*Look – a tortoiseshell brooch – look.*
*Look – a scab of dried mud – look.*
*Look – a dead leaf – look.*
*Look – an old fingerprint of blood – look.*

Stare unblinkingly
at the sand-and-bark
camouflage and suddenly
a bold calligraphy stares back.

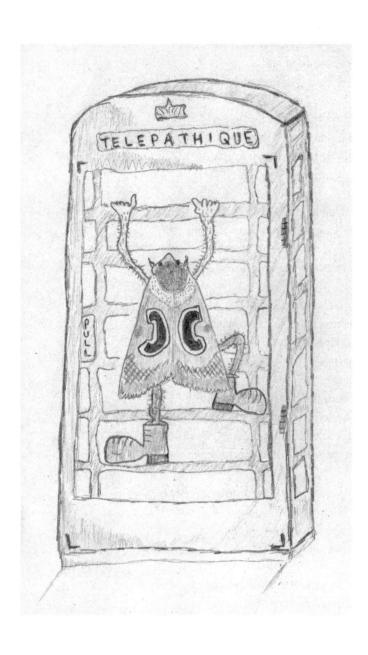

*Look – a tortoiseshell brooch – look.*
*Look – a scab of dried mud – look.*
*Look – a dead leaf – look.*
*Look – an old fingerprint of blood – look.*

But what are you doing *here*
on Eldon Street, your tawny robe
a single hand-drawn glyph
of primitive code

written in the year dot,
one scrap of windblown confetti
stained with an ink blot test, crouched
among overgrown graffiti.

In the battered kiosk
nothing connects to nowhere
and ripped wires
try to root in mid-air;

next to the headless telephone
your scripted pattern mouths
some silent essential word,
but meaning what, moth?

*Look – a tortoiseshell brooch – look.*
*Look – a scab of dried mud – look.*
*Look – a dead leaf – look.*
*Look – an old fingerprint of blood – look.*

Next to the banjaxed keypad
with its haywire maths
and garbled alphabet,
what are you saying, moth.

# Pleasure Fair

*(Register of Tenders and Attractions)*

If you're hoping for a peep show
at Barnsley Circus or some kind of freak show
– HOOPLA! – NOAH'S ARK! –

such as an ogre and an elf
tied together with a red scarf,
– THE FLYING CHAIRS! – DOBBY HORSES! –

like the pair
in Thomas Hardy's *At A Country Fair*,
– COCONUT SHY! – CAKE WALK! –

you'll come away disappointed. It features
no such creatures.
– SHOOTING GALLERY! – SPEEDWAY! –

Instead, two regular people brush hands
by the archery stall or candy floss stand,
– THE DODGEMS! – BEN HUR! –

both of them off their nuts on peanut brittle
and toffee apple,
– THE WALTZER! – THE AIRWAYS! –

and the ordinary boy
wins the everyday girl a cuddly toy.
– SIX DONKEYS! – AUTODROME! –

Then in the midnight black of the ghost train
they howl and scream
– BOXING RING! – DIVE BOMBER! –

when fake cobwebs trail over their faces,
and visit each others' secret places,
– CAROUSEL! – PENALTY KICK! –

till X many years later they're still *a thing*,
coupled together with long thin red string.
– BULLSEYE! – BUCKING BRONCO! –

# Promenade

And mother said
the Bunny Run
is where you'll hook
your honey bun.

And father said
the Bunny Run
is where you'll pluck
your sugar plum.

*So don't just stand there*
*sucking your thumb,*
*go on my girl,*
*get in my son.*
*Put your arse in gear.*
*But I waited there*
*till the day was done,*
*I waited there*
*till kingdom come.*

On Eldon Street
you'll meet your match.
Come Friday night
you'll catch your catch

when Barnsley's one big
amusement arcade,
where toys are grabbed
by clockwork cranes.

*So don't just stand there*
*sucking your thumb,*
*go on my girl,*
*get in my son.*
*Put your arse in gear.*
*But I waited there*
*till the day was done,*
*I waited there*
*till kingdom come.*

Colts and fillies
circle the town;
Barnsley's one big
merry-go-round.

And mother said
you'll soon get snagged,
you'll pull yourself
some likely lad.

Tickle a trout,
spear a whale,
catch a tiger
by the tail.

And father said
when they're tripping past
you're bound to snaffle
some lovely lass.

*So don't just stand there*
*sucking your thumb,*
*go on my girl,*
*get in my son.*
*Put your arse in gear.*
*But I waited there*
*till the day was done,*
*I waited there*
*till kingdom come.*

Smile and wink,
catch somebody's eye,
the human river
goes rolling by.

Hang out at hand
but fuck my luck
I was never much cop
at hook-a-duck.

Oh The Bunny Run,
The Bunny Run
where heads are turned
and dreams are spun.

The men revolve
and the women reel
and Barnsley's a living
Ferris Wheel.

# Sketch for Christ's Triumphal Entry into
   Eldon Street

¶ And they threw white roses at his feet, so the warm tarmac
   was strewn with white roses.

¶ Street cats and stray moggies knelt at his coming, their paws
   like Pomfret cakes.

¶ He signed autographs on a plastic football with a Sharpie,
   though with his left hand, for in his right he carried the lamb.

¶ In Melody House he struck a harmonious chord on a
   baby grand. The very sound of heaven, some said, still
   reverberating to this day.

¶ Coal dust would not settle on our Saviour's flowing white
   robes, but rolled away like rain from duck feathers.

¶ In Future Jeans he tried on a pair of bell-bottoms below his
   flowing white robes, and admired the snow-washed pre-
   distressed denim.

¶ And blessed the barrels of stout squatting like cross-legged
   wooden Buddhas in the beer cellar of the Devonshire Arms.

¶ And blessed the haddock and cod in Perkins Cudworth Fish
   Restaurant, making a witty aside about barley loaves.

¶ With a dip of his index finger he tasted the Pure Jams in
   Redman's Good Bacon Shop. The Dried Fruit he also found to
   his liking.

¶ Bad lads from the outskirts tossed Fun Snaps at his heels, and the police were called.

WATCHES, RINGS the clock said. The clock said WATCHES, RINGS

¶ He would not drink, but played pool with the lunchtime crowd in the snug of the Beer Engine, and tossed Roman coins into the upturned hat of a street busker outside the Acropolis Coffee Lounge.

¶ And turned his head momentarily to the flowing white robes in Betty's Costumer.

¶ His apostles were the 1912 FA Cup winning Tykes (plus substitute) in their home kit.

¶ And thence, like a little Jesus, came Amos the mascot astride his innocent donkey.

¶ In Swaddle's ironmongers a candle came spontaneously to life and shone fiercely in the Lord's bare hand.

¶ Christ as Belisha Beacon.

¶ Christ strobing black and white, black and white on the zebra crossing outside Saxone – 'Beautiful Shoes'.

¶ The shining black carriage horses lowered their heads. And lo! – Clara Shaw, tobacconist, offered Christ a ha'penny of snuff from the well of her hand. It could have been Kodiak, Longhorn, Rooster, Copenhagen, Husky, Timber Wolf, who knows.

¶ For the Old Match Box shall beget the Gaiety shall beget the Empire shall beget the Gaumont shall beget the Odeon shall beget the Parkway, for this is the way of life till kingdom come, and the show must go on.

¶ And he shook hands with dealers in fent.

WATCHES, RINGS the clock said. The clock said WATCHES, RINGS.

¶ He asked to see Her Majesty's Wedding Dress in Radiance bridal shop. And they knew not what to do, for it was on display in the Electricity Showrooms in faraway Huddersfield.

¶ The ragamuffins and urchins played thrutch against the solid door of the King's Head Stable Yard while our Lord Jesus prepared the bread.

¶ And Christ sayeth, 'Untie the shivering lurcher and bring him to me.'

¶ And turned his head momentarily to the flowing white robes in Scargill's Ladies Outfitters

¶ And to the Black Pudding King he said, 'He that bears the carcase shall wash his clothes, and be unclean until evening,' so that Albert purified himself in the drinking fountain outside the Cattle Market.

¶ He checked his reliable timepiece bought from Harral's, of course, lest he missed the last train to Meadowhall.

¶ A sachet of Pom-Pom Invigorator and a quart of Tommy Bottle Liniment were his chosen over-the-counter remedies in Holden's dispensing chemist.

¶ A skein of migrating barnacle geese from the Fleets honoured him with a flypast.

¶ For he spent a tenner in the .99p shop and said 'Keepeth the change' – such was his beneficence. Such was the size of his heart.

¶ In Warner Gothard's photographic postcard of the day, all that was captured on film was a dazzling blur of sunlight falling on fine white cloth.

WATCHES, RINGS the clock said. The clock said WATCHES, RINGS.

# The Proposal

I
Will you
be my wife?
Do you take
this knife?
The handle
is bone –
is that too weird?
I'm on bended knee.
Can you see
my smile
hanging upside down
in the stainless steel?
The serrated edge
will keep its bite.
Do you promise
to love me
slice after slice
after slice
after slice?
Time will stop
when the gold ball drops
on the time ball clock
in its fancy flask
of rounded glass –
it could be dawn
in Central Park,
it could be dusk
in Williamstown,
it could be Madrid,
Gdansk, Cadiz . . .

## II

Emerald, sapphire,
ruby, jet,
will you break
the bread,
will you be
my man
and hold this bread knife
by the hand,
spoil this bride
with butter and jam.
There'll be
bumps in the road
up ahead, up ahead,
we'll have to dodge
a runaway tram
and Indian elephants
nose to tail.
It could be Cape Town
Sydney, Deal.
Diamond, opal,
bloodstone, pearl:
precious stones
and wedding rings
but a bread knife's
the thing.
Now swear an oath:
will you be
my life,
will you be
my loaf?

# Unnatural History

Mountaineering up Eldon Street
through Pennine slush and Pennine sleet,
I met a man
with a two-headed lamb
with four brown eyes and a silver fleece.

He stopped me and said, 'When I went blind
it sang duets to soothe my mind
and kept me warm
from dusk to dawn.
No human creature was ever as kind.'

And the lamb looked left and the lamb looked right.

On Eldon Street, abseiling back down,
I met a woman riding through town
on a two-headed calf.
'When I went deaf,'
she said to me, 'this strange little cow

with its golden hide strolled through my door
and waltzed across my kitchen floor.
Then it nudged and nuzzled
with both its muzzles.
No actual person has loved me more.'

Then it sniffed the air to south and north.

When winter weather cuts me in half
or I swagger home as a bull or a ram

I remember the lamb and remember the calf,
and think twice about who I am.

DIVINE
GODDESS
OF
SOMETHING
OR
OTHER
DELIVERS
THE
CASKET
OF
VINYL

# Birthday

Tonight I'm Star Dust, Star Dust the aeroplane.

I carry five crew and six civilian passengers.

I'm one of the great unsolved aviation mysteries.

A streamline nymph loafs on my fuselage.

Iris is my 'Stargirl', my smiley flight attendant.

The volcano's name means 'star-viewpoint'.

I'm an Avro Lancastrian – a heavy contraption.

Clearer skies sunbathe at higher altitude.

Jet streams haven't yet entered my reckoning.

I'm freighted with human ashes and the King's Messenger.

STENDEC STENDEC – is that an anagram?

A mini avalanche is my swan song, my last aria.

Like a bear, understanding hunkers down and hibernates.

How long till the pilot's soft-shell helmet perishes?

Fifty blank years then suddenly I'm made manifest.

Lo and behold an aviation tyre remains inflated.

This severed hand bears traces of manicure.

A stowaway diamond stitched in a suit-lining: metaphor.

Where the glacier calves, the lost battalions assemble.

Climate change peels away decades of gift-wrapping.

Unfrozen, the mind's no black-box flight recorder.

I blow out the candles with a single extinction.


*(repeat lines in reverse order)*

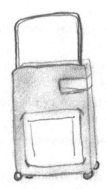

GREAT
UNSOLVED
AVIATION
MYSTERY

# Calling Card

I'm a presence here,
easing open the door, intruding under the eyes
of historical portraits and soft-toys.

Foreign and strange. A globe
in the window pulses its underhand code
from blue to crimson to green.

Nevertheless, how quickly this place,
undeniably yours, becomes mine:
the comfiest chair; that squeaking hinge

I should fix; where the corkscrew lives.
So before turning in I'm strolling
the long, low bridge

in the mural, casting bread
to the two becalmed swans,
trying it on with the red queen. *The red queen.*

The cushioned boudoir – that's where I'll sleep.
The stern governess, framed in gold,
turns the other cheek,

so in I go, and dream
with the panther's snout on my chest,
draped in a fun-fur pelt,

robed in the silk worm's beard.
Until morning stands by the bed,
and I haul

my old self out of the sheets,
and brush the crumbs of existence
into a paper bag, then walk out

backwards, erasing steps, resetting
the delicate structure of vacant air,
until I wasn't there. *I wasn't there.*

# Fishing Flies

Lanyard nation, placard nation. You're ticketed, laminated. You're franchised and mandated. You've got the last of the icebergs crying itself to sleep in the basement. Word for word you're a one-size-fits-all personal statement, you're pretty much word perfect. You're a golf sale, a free medium drink with every payment, you're the end of the world next Thursday. It's Wednesday and all your friends are screen-grabs and patents. You're contactless and trying to finesse the volcanic resentment. You're channelling the last albino tiger via indelible face paint. Narcissism wasn't your idea but, be honest, you've embraced it. Follow this link for the merch. Press hash to keep holding. Key in the first three words of your nearest station. Click here to prove you're still sentient. Say in a clear voice why you think you're worth it. So you're trying to be less carbon-dated this year and more pavement, but you're barefaced, you're blatant. You're thinking of trading it all for a needle and thread, to sit there vacant and patient until you've created . . . until you've created . . .

. . . the Dark Winged Olive Elk Hair Caddis and the Blue Damsel; the Detached Body Mayfly Spinner and the Royal Coachman; the Soft Hackle and the Banded Grasshopper and Tap's Popper; the Polar Shrimp and the Jock Scott and the Stoat's Tail and the Silver Zulu. And the Ace of Spades and the Mouserat and the Red Bloodfly Shipman's Buzzer. To work in silence under a clear light, to focus on feather and hook, looping and darning the Claret Heckham Peckham. And the Popsicle Streamer and the Grey Zonker and the White Wulff and the Egg Sucking Black Leech; the Yellow Tadpole and the Christmas Island Special and the Bearded Prince's Nymph and the Deepwater

White Gotcha. And the Mickey Finn and the Copper John. And the Thunder And Lightning. Enlightening.

# Heart for Sale

twilight quarter
backstreet corner
junk shop window
good working order

*heart for sale*
*open to offers*
*throw in a soul*
*one careless owner*

family heirloom
formaldehyde perfume
drop the grenade, son
let bygones be bygones

*heart for sale*
*open to offers*
*throw in a soul*
*one careless owner*

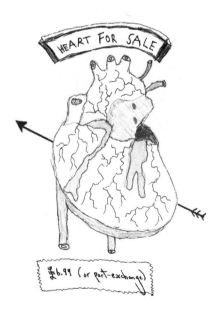

weasels they say
can wheedle their way
through eternity rings
and wormholes in space

*heart for sale*
*open to offers*
*throw in a soul*
*one careless owner*

# I'm Not Really a Waitress

Push open the door
of the wrong bedroom,
stalk through the spores
of heavy perfume.

There in the drawer
of the dressing table –
flaming desire
in a squat red bottle,

pearlescent and plush
and reeking of booze.
Dip the brush
in the slow red juice:

watch the fluid evolve
on the lacquered nail
as the pigments resolve
and the polymers heal.

All day it hardens
under your glove,
all night the enamel
will prove its love.

You have
      pierced the cherry,
      stoked the inferno,
      torched the Ferrari,
      primed the volcano.

You're wearing:
     I'm Not Really a Waitress,
     A Punctured Heart,
     Run Away with the Circus,
     Life On Mars.

## Living Legend

You've got the walk and the trademark sneer,
you're first at the vigil every year.
You lifted a blade of grass from his lawn,
stood barefoot on his grave at dawn.

You're chewing his half-chewed chewing gum
and keeping his plectrum under your thumb
and wearing his shades to see with his eyes.
His brothel creepers are just your size.

>   *And Lazarus came to the mouth of the cave*
>   *singing 'Lay Lady Lay'.*

You've got the quiff and the French cigarettes,
demos taped on vintage cassettes.
In his Afghan coat you're his living ghost,
slouched in the dive where he rolled his smokes.

Even his mother can't tell you apart –
you've got the B-sides off by heart,
you can forge his signature, do the voice,
(you've put more into it since the divorce . . .)

*And Lazarus came to the mouth of the cave*
*singing 'Purple Rain', singing 'Purple Haze'.*

>                 . . . thumbing a lift in the widow's hearse . . .
>                 . . . spouting his songbook chapter and verse . . .
>                 . . . stealing a quote from a dead man's lips . . .
>                 . . . outside Aldi, busking his hits . . .

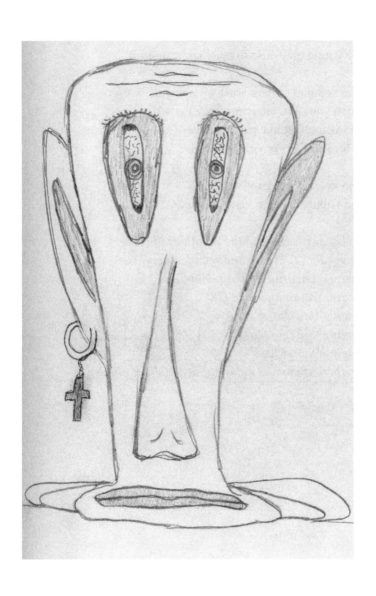

You've made a note of the concert rider:
the sturgeon roe, the Sumatran tiger,
the Himalayan mineral water,
the young masseuse to massage your aura . . .

And you don't give a stuff what anyone says
when you're re-enacting those early days,
all misunderstood, playing killer tunes
to broken seats in empty rooms.

And every cover band's a farce,
and tribute acts can kiss your arse.

*And Lazarus came to the mouth of the cave*
*plugged in, tuned up and ready to play,*
*singing 'Lazarus' and 'Aladdin Sane'*
*singing 'Anarchy in the UK'*
*singing 'Ancient of Days'*
*singing 'Maggie Mae'*
*singing 'Sweet Jane'*
*singing 'My way. I did it my way. I did it my way.'*

# Paradise Lost

Bonfire night –
all the windows in flames –
all the dogs on fire.
A blade of light
in the loading bay
of the superstore –
we limbo under
the roller-door –
sneak past the manager
counting his prize –
the gold doubloons
and denarii.

*Outside it's snowy*
*and comatose –*
*fifteen below –*
*twenty forty-five –*
*not a leaf on a tree –*
*not a bird in the sky . . .*

Enter the warehouse –
handle the products –
pocket the toys
from cereal boxes –
make a nest
among jars and cans –
bed down – stand up –
get engaged then hitched
in an Easter egg church –
raise a family there –
build a decent home

in the soap box suburbs –
in the neighbourhoods
of pallets and crates –
in the tea chest estates.

*Outside it's snowy*
*and comatose –*
*fifteen below –*
*twenty forty-five –*
*not a leaf on a tree –*
*not a bird in the sky . . .*

Once in a while
we stand on the roof
watching rockets explode –
seeing Alpha Centauri
and Machu Picchu
and Uluru
and the South Pole
and the Blue Pig
burning down to the ground.
Then it's time to leave –
the kids are grown up –
the candles snuffed –
the Żubrówka supped –
outside it's snowy
and comatose –
fifteen below –
twenty forty-five –
not a leaf on a tree –
not a bird in the sky . . .

# Presidentially Yours

The food tastes sweeter on a golden fork.
Golfing with God at noon, then let's talk.
Over broken bones the bald eagle soars.
Presidentially yours.

Love is . . . a large gun in a small hand.
Lizards salute the dragon's command.
Leave as you should have entered, on all fours.
Presidentially yours. Presidentially yours.

*Same thing – the sundial and the rotor blade.*
*Same thing – the cortege and the motorcade.*
*Same thing – the sundial and the rotor blade.*
*Same thing – the cortege and the motorcade.*

Candyfloss clings to the manicured claws.
Presidentially yours.

Whatever she said – didn't happen.
There's no shadow, just a spatter-pattern.
Kill the booing and roll the applause.
Presidentially yours.

*Same thing – the sundial and the rotor blade.*
*Same thing – the cortege and the motorcade.*
*Same thing – the sundial and the rotor blade.*
*Same thing – the cortege and the motorcade.*

137

Presidentially Yours ♪

She sweats like sweater on a golden john.
Gdyn will bod on Sundays, they flot filla.
Our spanired lowes the lay eagle sours.
Presidentially yours.

how is .... a Purje gus in a small band
higurds balts that & byons Cormorant
heare us go should have faticed, - on all faces
Presidentially yours.

Some thing - the sunbird with the odd blade.
Some thing & the cottege and the motorcnke
Cindy bloss sting to low manicured claws.
Presidentially yours.

Winter she said - didn't huppen.
There's no shadows, just a sparkle-gettero
till the townie and all the applant.
Presidentially yours.

## Seasons Out of Phase

Tune the dial for better days,
coastal strips and country lanes,
Pyrenees or Everglades?
        Ultraviolet waves.

Fingers blue with blackberries,
the silence of the factories,
Tuesday's where the action is,
        seasons out of phase.

        Party hats from paper maps,
        the bell rings for the final lap,
        I'm walking home on bubble wrap . . .

Rollerblade the interstate,
execute a figure eight
on roller skates like razor blades.
        The ultraviolet age.

Dirty coins and magazines,
get slutty with the slot machines,
snowplough round putting greens,
        seasons out of phase.

Paper kites and evergreens,
open skies and purple dreams,
count the hours in coffee beans,
        ultraviolet haze.

Swerve the pharaoh's motorcade,
free the summer from its cage,

meet me at the kissing-gate,
    seasons out of phase.

    Party hats from paper maps,
    the bell rings for the final lap,
    I'm walking home on bubble wrap . . .

Margaritas in the veins,
then poking fun at aeroplanes,
then skinny-dipping August rain,
    ultraviolet days.

Open up the neighbourhood,
the bat's no longer in our blood,
your brand new shoes are looking good,
    seasons out of phase.

Music drives a passing car,
light years from the nearest star,
FYI it's LYR,
    the ultraviolet age.

# To the Fashion Industry in Crisis

And I apologise for my ungainly external appearance
my sweet lord,
your all-seeing eye saw me Pritt-stick a Lamborghini badge
to an off-the-peg Ford.
And I'm sincerely sorry for looking this way I'm not usually
the slovenly kind
but I'd set my heart on a dark night of the soul when somebody
threw back the blind.

I'd been arm-wrestling with JD and the Holy Ghost
on the overgrown lawn,
then me and JB were trading Oblique Strategies
through until dawn.
Now I'm window shopping for glimmers of self-esteem
and sticking it all on a card,
now I'm dialling Deliveroo, ASOS and Amazon Prime
on a dyslexic Ouija board.

So I chose badly when I fell for the supermodel
with the pop-a-matic heart
but frankly I'm a shopaholic whose got getting suckered
down to a fine art.
What's the word for being simultaneously enthralled
and appalled by your own likeness?
What's the cure for being dazzled by page after blank page
of snow blindness?

Me and JD doing naked online all-night poker to a soundtrack
of bad luck;
JB leading me down the overgrown primrose path
with a sippy cup;

yours truly playing Cards Against Humanity
into the small hours, solitaire version;
guess who presenting himself in the gold-rimmed vanity
mirror in person!

I'm my own target audience, the trophy cupboard's groaning
with third prizes.
I'm an influencer touting five hundred quid paisley wellies –
which is priceless
when I'm trying to compose a twisted love letter
to the fashion industry in crisis
but I'm sidetracked by white noise and static and deafening
radio silence.

*Pat in his wooden shack under the clouds and stars.*
*Rich in his glorified garden shed with his weeping guitars.*
*Simon on Scammonden footbridge counting the cars.*

I blew my first million on a rip-off Dior Gucci Armani
string vest,
and that Instagram pout I've been paying for in instalments
has gone west;
I've got a pug in my clutch-bag, I'm flaunting limited edition
zebra skin Docs,
so if I put both feet on the seat opposite is that, like,
punk rock?

# THREE WEATHER SONGS

# i New Neighbours

They'd come from somewhere north. No garden gnomes,
just mouldy curtains, a van slouched in the street
like an old boat, sulky kids with odd names:
      Rain, Hail, Snow, Sleet.

Mudbath lawn – a graveyard of spent fridges.
Through the spindly hedge I watched the freak show
of their summer picnic, bowls of . . . delicious
      Rain, Sleet, Hail, Snow.

Even in cloudbursts and hard frost they hung
grey bedsheets on the line like tattered sails.
The shipping forecast moaned its sorry song:
      Rain, Snow, Sleet, Hail.

## ii  More Rain

We certainly had more heat. Fahrenheit
    salted away in the stone and the grain,
more tan on the skin, seasons of sheer light
    for cavorting in. But we had more rain
       *and down from heaven it came.*

We had more gizmos and toys, devices
    under our fingers, no need for the brain
to put in a long shift, we had licence
    to crack mountains like eggs. But still more rain
       *and over the earth it came.*

And more time – more hours to clock up the miles.
    We refuelled mid-flight by glugging champagne
straight from the nozzle, kept spinning the dials
    and surfing the rising tide. Still more rain
       *and up out of hell it came.*

More Rain

We certainly had much heat, Fahrenheit
sulted and [...] the [...] and the grain,
more than [...] the [...] seasons of [...] light
for cultivating. But we had more rain,
and [...] from heaven it came.

We had more grasses and tone, devoirs
[...] us [...], no said for the rain
to [...] in [...] day, we had because
to [...] [...] and eggs. But more rain,
and over the earth it came.

And more time [...] [...] to clear up the [...]
We [...] and [...] to be [...] [...]
[...] from the [...], [...] again [...]
and [...] the rising tide [...] more rain,
and [...] et up [...] to come.

rain, hail, sleet and snow          x
rain, snow, hail and sleet          x
rain, sleet, snow and hail

## iii Herons

The matter of Britain being stained with water,
herons have stalked inland from the ponds and lakes,
bold now against England's planted borders.
    This one's a weathervane,
this one's cloaked in an old photographer's cape.

Away from brushwood nests beaconed in lanky trees,
a rickety tripod of bill and legs
haunts a garden puddle; amber eyes peer
    straight through the mirror
of yesterday's rain into summer's dregs.

New breeds of winged space-telescope unfold;
herons fix on pinholes of ancient light, spy
on far galaxies at their feet, find untold
    life-giving planets
and the first stars, then stab holes in the sky.

# Country Club Revisited (Hurricane Mix)

The sommelier loosens a champagne cork.
The mile-long limos are rolling up.
Candlelight splinters from polished forks.
A row of roof tiles has come unstuck.

Storm clouds gather, blacken, thicken.
A fanfare announces the seventh course:
it's a stuffed partridge stuffed in a chicken,
stuffed in a turkey, stuffed in a horse. . .

On the guest list:
    Hurricane Betty and Hurricane Blake,
    Hurricane Jackie and Hurricane Jake,
    Hurricane Humphrey and Hurricane Hannah,
    Hurricane Sam and Hurricane Susannah.

Sea spray lashes the promenade.
Sea trout flounder in taxi ranks.
A car is hurtled a hundred yards.
A simmering grudge has burst its banks.

Uprooted trees have blocked the roads.
A yacht crash-lands on somebody's lawn.
It's snowing gravel, it's raining toads.
The kid on the coat desk stifles a yawn.

    *There's a cyclone swirling in Hector's eye,*
    *a whirlwind waiting on Ruby's tongue,*
    *tornadoes brewing in Jeremy's mind;*
    *the crème brûlée is underdone.*

The candle-snuffer has made his rounds.
Milk floats have floated away on the tide.
Spent expletives litter the grounds.
The whole of a mountain begins to slide.

On the guest list:
> Hurricane Trudy and Hurricane Tyler,
> Hurricane Tammy and Hurricane Taylor,
> Hurricane Zack and Hurricane Zoe,
> Hurricane Clive and Hurricane Chloe,
> Hurricane Bathsheba and Hurricane Barrett,
> Hurricane Juliet and Hurricane Jarrett,
> Hurricane Arthur and Hurricane Amanda,
> Hurricane Miles and Hurricane Miranda.

> Hurricane Tom and Hurricane Tilly,
> Hurricane Morgan and Hurricane Millie,
> Hurricane Tallulah and Hurricane Tristan,
> Hurricane Kirk and Hurricane Kristen,
> Hurricane Timothy and Hurricane Tate,
> Hurricane Karl and Hurricane Kate,
> Hurricane Greg and Hurricane Gabby,
> Hurricane Archie and Hurricane Abbey,
> Hurricane Lottie and Hurricane Louis,
> Hurricane Hattie and Hurricane Hughie.

# Gravel

*Quarry the rolling corn,*
*harvest the liquid stone,*
*carry the treasure home.*

Come down to the river,
stand on its bare shoulder,
ditch the umbrella,
dip your soul in the water.

There, under the bank
where the sand martins skulk,
buckets of earth-money,
geological honey.

*Quarry the rolling corn,*
*harvest the liquid stone,*
*carry the treasure home.*

Grains of fire in the embers,
a fleck of blue cinder
still asleep in your flesh
where it came to rest.

Hard to believe each piece
was a whole planet once.
That's a lie by the way,
gravel is sun-struck rain.

*Quarry the rolling corn,*
*harvest the liquid stone,*
*carry the treasure home.*

Let's hoodwink the driver,
hot-wire the bulldozer
and open the planet's door
with the big yellow claw.

No, these nuggets of light
aren't ours to keep;
steal back to the stream
and tip out the gold seeds.

# Guernica Jigsaw

He works in the sweat lodge
of the gallery gift shop,
staggers out punch-drunk
for a half-hour lunch break.

Then roams the Zen gardens
of the gentrified margins,
strolls through riotous petals
forged from recycled metals.

*Who will buy my Guernica jigsaw?*
*Who will buy my Mondrian stress ball?*

*Basquiat skateboard,*
*Lichtenstein snow globe,*
*Oven glove Kahlo,*
*Shower cap Rothko.*

*What's not to love – the Brancusi lampshade.*
*What's not to love – the Kandinsky phone case.*

The store she works in
sells Paisley and snakeskin.
She thinks vintage thoughts
among camel hair coats.

They pass on the escalators
between Argos and Specsavers,
fazed by abstract sculpture
in the City of Culture.

# Let's Bird-Table

Take the weight off, comrade,
good to eyeball with you,
we could drill down
into some core digits,
I could tell you those witchetty grubs
are chicken nuggets,
it's a blue ocean out there,
but what does it look like
on a clear day from Kilimanjaro?
Sorry to throw open
the fluffy bath robe, captain,
but you're circling the drain
if you speak my language,
all sizzle and no sausage, chief.
I can send you the screen grab
or the stone commandment
but the white gloves don't lie,
it's a simple case
of seven shoes and one octopus.
I'm telling you, padre,
there's a hundred million mouse-potatoes
out there in cube-land
all sniffing the same poodle.
So what's your order,
filet mignon or the Sheffield salad?
See where I'm sailing, soldier?
I'll give you the off-brand
one-size-fits-all version:
don't try to swallow
the whole brontosaurus
or you'll die on the hill

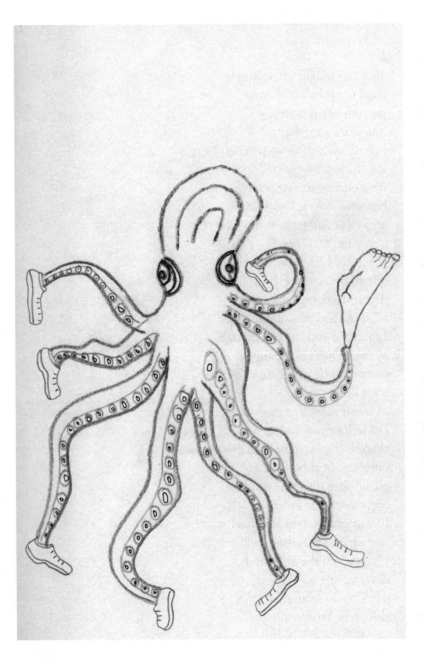

and won't move the needle.
Let me tell you, sergeant,
at the blame-storming session
your weevil came out of the biscuit;
even the snout-casts at ground zero
are stubbing out ciggies
in your sand-bucket.
It's Thatcher versus Thatcher
out there, commando,
time to take off your tights
and mend the fan belt,
you don't want choirboys
under lawnmower
and I don't either.
Are we touching knees on this,
shall we squeeze the sponge, private,
or are we painting the bathroom
so the Queen of the Nile
can come for Christmas?
Tell you what, slide by one day
and we'll chop some logs;
me and a few amigos
like to ride bareback
all the way to hotel mojito,
so saddle up, son, let's bird-table.

# Mile High Club

I waved at the newlyweds
sailing above me in a hot air balloon,
the puffball bride
and the pinstripe groom.

*The heart afloat, the heart in ropes.*

I swear I could smell the propane,
hear the flexing leather
and creaking wicker
when they laid down together.

*The heart afloat, the heart in ropes.*

'Watch out for thorns,' I semaphored,
'the spiky bouquet and the prickly wreath.'
They threw a rose overboard
which I caught in my teeth.

*The heart afloat, the heart in ropes.*

'If we capsize,' the man thundered,
'we'll parachute down
in the bloated meringue
of her jelly-fish gown.'

*The heart afloat, the heart in ropes.*

'If we crash-land,' the woman yelled,
'my well-dressed husband

has promised me
we'll be well-cushioned.'

*The heart afloat, the heart in ropes.*

Gods of the isotherms,
would you really tamper
with a couple honeymooning
in their own picnic hamper?

Let them ride the contours
of a rough century,
drifting through mountains of thick cloud
to the fields of Eventually.

# Sirius

If we're both old hands
    at judging distance
then the perfect range
    is touching distance.
*Sidebar*: in the end what keeps us
    face-to-face
isn't naked attraction
    but personal space.

And look how we keep on
    finding strength
by holding each other
    at arm's length.
*Bullet point*: the emptiness
    has to be razor thin
for static to leap
    from skin to skin.

*Just nanometres*
*standing between us;*
*Sirius alpha, Sirius beta, Sirius alpha, Sirius beta . . .*
   *(serious business)*

The zodiac traipses
    around its circuit;
the Dog Star dances
    in captured orbit.
*In brackets:* across the divide
    you can feel the tension:
it's love, alright –
    in the fifth dimension.

We should fall apart,
    but the thing that saves us –
*write this in CAPS* –
    is spatial awareness.
*Footnote*: there's no chemistry here –
    it's pure electricity;
no contact allowed –
    just high-voltage proximity.

# Snow Day

I call it sniper's alley you call it the pavement.
You call it the dawn chorus I call it aerial bombardment.

I just needed a snow day.
A go slow day.
An Alamo day.
A living in my own private Idaho day.
I just needed a snow day.

I see double agents you see market traders.
You see triple rainbows I see space invaders.

I just needed a think day.
A blue-tongued skink day.
A me and the kitchen sink day.
A pull back from the brink day.
I just needed a think day.

I say Novichok you say herbs and spices.
You say hollyhocks I say listening devices.

I just needed a head day.
An all day in bed day.
A nothing said day.
A rainwater and dry bread day.
I just needed a head day.

For snake oil read frankincense.
For the-eyes-as-the-windows-of-the-soul read artificial
    intelligence.

For drone read red kite.
For rush hour read red alert.

So thanks for asking but today's a no no no no no day.
I just needed a snow day.

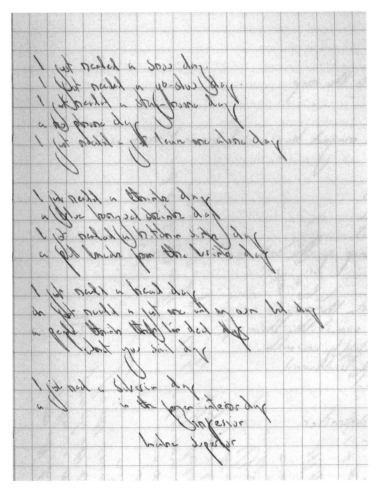

# Tried in the Court of Public Opinion

I said a word.
   It was overheard.
      My name is dirt.

   *

I was tried in the court
   of public opinion,
pierced to the core,
   skewered and pinioned
by the merciless thoughts
   of anonymous millions,
banished from the shores
   of the great dominions.

   *

I said a word.
   It was overheard.
      My name is dirt.

      Now I say it more
   than I did before
(but behind closed doors).

   *

I was tried in the court
   of public opinion,
trolled and stalked
   by righteous civilians

who'd heard reports
    of my forked tongue. Reptilian,
I'm exiled to the north
    of the far pavilions.

# Do We Really Care #2

I'm curious,

because to show mercy once in a blue moon only makes
the unforgiving more furious,

as if kindness and grace were ethereal rare gifts in the realm
of the luxurious,

as if there were something hard and remote at the core
of the human nucleus,

despite compassion and tenderness making the darkest of souls
almost perfectly luminous.

I've sensed some creature not far from the surface, cold-blooded,
imperious,

with a heart like a cannonball lost in an ocean trench, stony,
impervious,

or lodestone lodged in the brain and locked on a bad star
that brings out the worst in us.

Look at me, God's gift to graffiti, spellchecking
'injurious';

look at you, joy-riding the soft-top hearse all the way
to the terminus;

here we go, planting our poppies then torching the forest,
carelessly serious.

Meanwhile we're crowding the brink of the lip of the cusp
of the rim of the next Vesuvius,

trying to flag down a passing planet or mother-ship, failing
to lip-read the universe.

# Killing Balloons

The party's over, morning has yawned.
Neuorofen breakfast, ash-tray thoughts.
Head on the cushion, brain like a stone.
Three dead men button their coats

and leave.

> And I'm on my own, hands in my sleeves.
> And here are balloons, bags of old breath.
> Sad little lungs, small purses of life.
> Sharpen a knife.

Remember the rabbit girl who drowned?
All that she left – an inflatable moon.
Remember the boy, breathing her in
day after day after the boat went down.

The show's over, the house lights are up.
Lipstick smudged on a plastic cup.
Tickets dropped on the stairs and the street.
Three black taxis square the circle

and leave.

> And I'm on my own, hands in my sleeves.
> And here are balloons, bags of old breath.
> Sad little lungs, small purses of life.
> Sharpen a knife.

# London

You saw my dad on the overground platform
dressed in your second best Lurex mini skirt . . .

I saw your mother at the all-night bus stop
flaunting a nightie that was my old school shirt . . .

What they say about strange mister Freud
is he knew one or two things about why the heart hurts.

*London,*
*all stories and scenes;*
*there's someone*
*I'd like you to meet.*

*London, the dream's*
*in sight;*
*marry me please*
*tonight.*

Hooked a book through the mouth of a book bank,
crashed for an hour in a clapped-out coffee shop.

Watched my reflection stroll through a glasshouse,
pinged you a text that was nine-tenths poppycock.

You said, 'You can keep on going
till I tell you to stop,' and I said 'COPY THAT'.

What's love? Margaritas at dawn
and a stranger's lips in the back of an Uber.

Got hitched in a multi-storey car park
nine floors high looking out to the future . . .

# Taxi to Comeback Street

I found you underneath the fire escape,
not really alive.
Your faded Triple A laminate
expired in '95.

I dragged you back to my maisonette
through pale winter sun.
You crashed out like a marionette
with all its strings undone.

*Fallen hero, fallen idol*
*in the house of your disciple –*
*let's get you back on your feet.*

*Fallen hero, fallen idol,*
*now's the hour of your revival –*
*taxi to Comeback Street.*

I propped you up on the breakfast bar,
shaved, showered and dressed.
Rode you around in a soft-top car
until you decompressed.

I still treasure that poster of you
from before the great fall.
You watched me doing what teenagers do
from my bedroom wall.

*Fallen hero, fallen idol*
*in the house of your disciple –*
*let's get you back on your feet.*

*Fallen hero, fallen idol,*
*now's the hour of your revival –*
*taxi to Comeback Street.*

You don't need some phoney TikTok account
for notoriety.
You won't be stashing some monster amount
in crypto currency.

You made a nation's pacemaker stop
with your Marilyn pout.
Art school rock versus bubble-gum pop
is what it's all about.

. . . grab your guitar and take my arm,
. . . let's hit the road to Worthy Farm . . .

# Under Artificial Lighting

So I'm out on patrol
on a hunt for the soul
of the nation.

Or I'm cruising the sky
to piss in the eye
of creation.

A rocking horse skitters
through battlefields littered
with jawbones;

I'll climb on its back
and follow the track
to the war zones.

But I do my best writing
under artificial lighting.

'Get off your arse
and make yourself sparse –
that's an order.'

So I'm dragging my feet
along Centipede Street
to the border.

'March to the drum,
get a wriggle on, son.'
I'm the loafer

who's staying afloat
in a storm-battered boat
on the sofa.

I'm just far more exciting
under artificial lighting.

*. . . in the bedroom window . . .*
*. . . there's a neon flamingo . . .*

Get you, Mr Benn,
you're an astronaut then
a lion tamer.

But all the best tunes
are here in this room –
it's a no brainer.

I'll kick back and stew
with a fag and a brew,
contemplating.

Leave the world be,
let the stars come to me,
I'll be waiting.

Look the morning's brightening
under artificial lighting.

OUTRO

## *Feltham Sings* (Channel 4, 2002)

A musical documentary directed by Brian Hill for Century Films. Music by Dextrous. Based on their own stories and circumstances, the lyrics were written to be performed by inmates at Feltham Young Offender Institution in West London. Each wing of the prison is named after a bird, and the grounds are home to dozens of semi-domesticated peacocks. The film received a Best Documentary BAFTA and an Ivor Novella Award for Best Original Music for Television.

## *Songbirds* (2005, Channel 4)

A musical documentary directed by Brian Hill for Century Films. A follow up to *Feltham Sings*, set in Downview Prison for women in Sutton. Music by Simon Boswell. Prior and subsequent to transmission the work was screened internationally at several film festivals including Sundance, Sarajevo and Leipzig.

## *Born in a Barn*, The Scaremongers (album, Corporation Pop, 2009)

'Cardigan Girl' is the only complete song I have written on my own, by which I mean I composed both the lyrics and the tune.

## *I Am Thomas*, Told by an Idiot (2016)

Directed by Paul Hunter, a co-production with the National Theatre of Scotland and Royal Lyceum Edinburgh, in association with Liverpool Everyman and Playhouse. Music by Iain Johnstone. A musical theatre piece telling the story of Thomas Aikenhead, the last person in Britain to be executed for blasphemy.

*Call in the Crash Team*, LYR (album, Mercury KX, 2020)

'33 1/3' was originally written as a poem commemorating the death of Ian Curtis. The LYR track samples the crackly run-out groove from side 2 (The 'Outside') ('THIS IS THE WAY') of Joy Division's *Unknown Pleasures* album.

A version of 'Great Coat' was written to be set to music by Stephen Fretwell. It never (as far as I know) happened.

'Leaves on the Line' was originally commissioned as a song lyric to be set to music and performed by the King's Singers at a royal concert at the time of the millennium. Never happened.

'Never Good with Horses' was written for a late Marianne Faithful album, to be set to music by Tom McRae. Never happened.

'The National Trust Range of Paints Colour Card' was first published in *Travelling Songs* (Faber & Faber, 2002).

'Urban Myth #91' was written for a BBC live broadcast event from Gateshead Baltic under the title *A Tree Full of Monkeys*, with music by Zoviet France.

'Zodiac T-Shirt' was written for performance at Beck's *Song Reader* show at London's Barbican Centre in 2013, and first published in *Sandettie Light Vessel Automatic* (Faber & Faber, 2019).

## LYR, Singles and EPs

Originally a 'laureate poem', 'Lockdown' was written near the beginning of the Covid-19 pandemic and set to music about six months later. The first section refers to the outbreak of bubonic plague in the Derbyshire village of Eyam in 1665, the second section recalls elements of the Meghadūta ('Cloud Messenger'), the epic Sanskrit poem by the Indian poet Kālidāsa (c.4th–5th CE). All profits from the record went to the charity Refuge in recognition of the increased cases of domestic abuse reported during lockdown. The finished track featured a vocal by Florence Pugh and a saxophone solo from Pete Wareham of Melt Yourself down.

'Winter Solstice': the phrase 'Desire as a sylph-figured creature who changes her mind' is taken from Prefab Sprout's song 'Desire As', from their 1985 album *Steve McQueen*, and used with their blessing. Prefab Sprout vocalist Wendy Smith made a spoken word recording of the line for use on 'Winter Solstice', for which we are forever grateful.

## *We'll Sing*, Huddersfield Choral Society (2021)

Two lyrics commissioned by my local, world-famous choir, and set to music by Cheryl Frances-Hoad ('We'll Sing') and Daniel Kidane ('The Song Thrush and the Mountain Ash'). Lockdown had been particularly cruel in relation to those art forms requiring live participation, and doubly so in the case of choirs, in a world where both congregating and singing had been made unlawful due to fears about the spread of infection. At a time when the Society had already lost two of its members through Covid-19, both pieces were recorded remotely or with social-distancing measures in place, and directed by Greg Batsleer. The songs featured in the BBC Film *Where Did the World Go, A Pandemic Poem* (2021, Century Films), directed by Brian Hill.

## *Firm As a Rock We Stand*, LYR (2022)

An LYR commission from Durham Brass Festival and Durham Miners' Association to write and perform a suite of work exploring County Durham's Category D villages. In the 'fifties and 'sixties, following the slow decline of the coal industry, two local authority development plans gave all mining villages in the county an A to D classification. Those categorised as D – over a hundred and twenty by the final reckoning – were deemed as economically hopeless and ear-marked for eventual demolition, with no further investment or development to take place. Left to wither on the vine, most villages struggled on through a combination of self-determination and bloody-mindedness. But at least four were wiped off the face of the map, including Addison, on the banks of the Tyne, and Marsden, on the coast next to the Souter Lighthouse. Five tracks, arranged by Simon Dobson, were recorded with a brass band from a different Marsden – Marsden in West Yorkshire, the village where I grew up. I saw this as an act of solidary and kinship between two communities of the same name, one lending its voice to the other, a sort of kiss-of-life exercise through the blowing of brass instruments. The pieces were performed in Durham Cathedral with Easington Colliery Band as part of the 2022 Durham Brass weekend. The EP title is taken from the Marsden Lodge Banner, the union banner of the nearby colliery, depicting Marsden Rock, a natural limestone arch in the sea that partially collapsed in the mid-nineties following successive winter storms. With special thanks to Sue Collier and Ross Forbes.

## *Barnsley – An Unnatural History*, LYR (2022)

Commissioned as a Heritage Action Zone project, LYR composed a suite of music commemorating and celebrating Eldon Street, one of Barnsley's main thoroughfares, and home to hundreds of different shops and emporiums over the years. The work took as its starting point a partly forgotten and near-legendary Natural History Museum that once existed in the town, which at some point had been dismantled and its exhibits discarded. Flauna and flora run riot through the lyrics, along with issues of local history, urban decay and urban renewal. Presented as a kind of visiting carnival, circus or fair, the project culminated with a live performance at the Parkway Cinema that featured an accompanying film by James Lockey. With special thanks to Dominic Somers and Tegwen Roberts.

'Hebrew Character': the moth *Orthosia gothica*.

'Promenade': the Bunny Run is a Barnsley tradition dating from the 'forties and 'fifties. On Sunday evenings young men and women would promenade in a circuit round the town centre, sometimes in opposite directions, hoping to catch someone's eye and perhaps meet the love of their life. The phrase is still used today but as a more general term for a night on the town or a pub-crawl.

'The Proposal': couples who bought their wedding rings from Benj Harral's jewellers on Eldon Street were given a complimentary bread knife with the words 'Wishing You Both Every Happiness' engraved on the blade. The shop boasted a 'time ball' in a semi-circular window on the first floor, a device usually associated with coastal settlements to signal the hour to vessels at sea.

'Unnatural History': the two-headed lamb and the two-headed calf can be found in the Cawthorne Victoria Jubilee Museum.

## *The Ultraviolet Age*, LYR (album, forthcoming)

An early version of 'Calling Card' was first published in *The Motorway Service Station as a Destination in its Own Right* (Smith/Doorstop Books, 2009).

'I'm Not Really a Waitress' is the name of a 'Chianti red' nail lacquer by OPI. In 2021, during lockdown, LYR were asked to choose from a range of colours selected by David Hockney and write a one-minute song based on that particular shade or tone. A short film would then be made using the music as a soundtrack. Never happened.

## *Three Weather Songs*

Composed following a tentative enquiry by the Pleyel Ensemble (violin, cello, piano) for a song-cycle on a contemporary theme to be sung by a tenor. Jumping the gun somewhat, my idea was to feed that classic British conversation topic – the weather – through the filter of climate change. Or to stage issues of environmentalism within different domestic settings.

## Miscellaneous

'Do We Really Care #2': a contribution to the *12 Questions* album by Future Utopia, the solo project by 'super-producer' Fraser T Smith, featuring Dave, Kojey Radical, Kano, Arlo Parks, Tom Grennan and others. The lyric, in my own voice on the record (and recorded at home as an iPhone Voice message), was written in response to the provocation Do We Really Care?

'Killing Balloons': written for and performed by Tom McRae.

'London': written for Will Taylor/Flyte.

'Taxi to Comeback Street': written for Will Taylor/Flyte.

'Under Artificial Lighting': written for Guy Garvey.

# Acknowledgements

Thanks are due to Domino Publishing for their kind permission in the reproduction of these lyrics, to LYR, and to LYR manager Alex Zinovieff.

Many thanks to Craig Smith of The Scaremongers. The division of labour in that band was never analysed or formalised, though I think we would both agree that for the most part he took charge of the music and I assumed an unspoken responsibility for the lyrics. Nevertheless, certain lines and phrases, some of them going back to our student days, came from his lips and his hand. Where they appear in this book, I'm grateful for his nod of approval.

# Index of Titles